"This book is simply awesc
—*The Vermont Cynic, Un.*

**"A welcome celebration of inebriation
and human silliness."**
—*All About Beer Magazine*

"A complete manual for party animals."
—*Bartender Magazine*

"A classic guide to raucous fun."
—*Playboy*

"The definitive coffee-table book for college
students."—*The Torch, St. John's Univ.*

"You can only drink 30 or 40
glasses of beer a day,
no matter how rich you are."
—*Col. Adolphus Busch*

REVISED & EXPANDED!

BEER GAMES 2

THE EXPLOITATIVE SEQUEL

Andy Griscom • Ben Rand
Scott Johnston • Michael Balay

Mustang Publishing
Memphis, TN

Picture Credits: p. 7, John Mongillo/Jackson Newspapers; p.25, Louisiana State Museum; pp. 40, 71, & 136, Superstock; pp. 72-91 & 144, Rollin A. Riggs; p. 100, Universal Studios.

Drawings on pages 15, 30, 38, 45, 57, 94, 104, 128, & 132 by **SEAN KELLY**.

PUBLISHER'S NOTE: Excessive alcohol consumption is very dangerous and can lead to sickness and even death. Neither the publisher nor the authors encourage excessive alcohol consumption, and we accept no liability for the consequences of your behavior if you overindulge. Drink responsibly; don't be an idiot; and don't blame us if you crash your car or puke your guts out.

Library of Congress Cataloging in Publication Data

Beer games 2: the exploitative sequel / Andy Grisom ... [et al.]. -- Rev. & expanded.
     p.   cm.
   Rev. ed. of: Beer games II. c1986.
   Continues: The complete book of beer drinking games / Andy Griscom, Ben Rand, Scott Johnston. Rev. & expanded. c1994.
    ISBN 0-914457-67-5 (acid-free paper) : $8.95
   1. Drinking games--United States. 2. Beer--Humor. I. Griscom, Andy, 1960- . II. Griscom, Andy, 1960- Complete book of beer drinking games. III. Beer games II. IV. Title: Beer games two.
GV1202.D74B44 1995
793.2--dc20   94-32647
                                     CIP

Printed on acid-free paper.
10 9 8 7 6 5 4 3 2

*Dedicated to everyone
who has written to the
Beer Research Department*

Acknowledgments

Without a doubt, the people who deserve the most thanks are all the dedicated beer gamesters who sent new games, advice, and encouragement to our notorious Beer Research Department. If it weren't for them, we would have actually had to *work* on this book, and that's almost unthinkable.

Some other people who deserve a big thank you include Tot Hufstader, Vaughan Easter, Mike Kelly, Oscar Huettner, Michael Shavelson (wherever he may be), Mark Harris, Mike Natan, Debbie Mercer, Lawrence Wilkins, Joy Harris, Sara Robbins, Sharon Irwin, Hillary and Lauren, Eliza and Ellery, Jim Buffum, Ed Winkle, Kelly Schmidt, Chris and John Rand, Doc-oh Burke, Al 'Memo' Austin, Josh Groves, Jeff Seeley, Deborah Daly, Mara Lavitt, Clair Stamatien, Tamara Bozof, Rollin Riggs, Ryan Riggs, Allison Christian, and Spock and Kirk the Wonder Cats.

DON'T BE STUPID

Alcohol is a dangerous drug. And, like it or not, it's an illegal drug in America if you're under 21.

Alcohol will severely impair your reflexes, and if you try to drive when you're drunk, you stand a good chance of killing yourself or murdering someone else. Here's a sickening statistic: Among people age 16-24, alcohol-related car wrecks are **the leading cause of death**.

Don't be stupid. Don't abuse alcohol. Don't drink and drive, and don't let your friends drink and drive, either. Use the designated driver system, or call a cab, or just crash on a convenient sofa.

Look, if you want to kill yourself, do everyone a favor and play with a toaster in the bathtub. Just don't drive drunk.

CONTENTS

PREFACE

BEER GAMES: THE UNTOLD STORY

Okay, we know what you're thinking: A sequel? More beer games? Who are these guys kidding, anyway? And why, if our first book was called *The **Complete** Book of Beer Drinking Games*, do we have more games now? What, we lied the first time?

Well, we agree that it's annoying when writers devise a sequel to a book that claimed to be complete in the first place. But to give you an idea of why we *had* to write this sequel, let's look at some of the things we've had to do since our first book appeared. Among the more onerous tasks our ogre of a publisher foisted upon us were publicity tours that involved judging wet T-shirt contests (we really hated that), TV talk shows that required us to play Beer Hunter with gorgeous hostesses, and personal appearances to greet countless adoring fans. And fawning women, too. Lots of them. Really.

Now, you're probably thinking: Hey, that sounds awesome! Well, you're right. It's great! So wouldn't we be foolish if we didn't try to keep a good thing going? In fact, we could keep doing this for years. Granted, having people tear out locks of our hair and rip our clothes off in public might get a little old, but other than that, no problem.

Also, you see, by writing another incredibly immature book, all we're doing is prolonging our adolescence. And getting paid to do it, too. Heh, heh.

And speaking of money, do you realize that we can legally deduct all the beer we buy?! Nightclub cover charges, too! Is this a great country, or what?

Besides, everybody loves our first book (except for a few self-righteous buttheads). A lot of the games have really caught on, and so has some of our terminology, such as the now-ubiquitous word "boot" and the dreaded "Lotrium." Furthermore, our commentaries on the politics and ethos of beer drinking have proved sage. We said that when America feels good about itself, it drinks beer, and when America drinks beer, it feels good about itself. Well, who won the Cold War—the country that invented light beer, or the country that invented bad vodka?

So we proudly present *Beer Games 2: The Exploitative Sequel,* and the relentless march of depravity will continue. For in this expanding universe of uncivilized knowledge, we, the authors, are merely pawns.

Damn happy pawns, though.

Andy Griscom   Ben Rand   Scott Johnston   Michael Balay

Introduction:
Is There Beer after College?

When we first put pen to paper to write a book, we were all in college. That alone made writing difficult, and the fact that we had to conduct exhaustive "research" on our topic made things nearly impossible. For instance, try writing anything coherent after investigating the topic "Is God Still Dead after 10 Pitchers?". (No, incidentally, He's not. You see Him several times. You even talk to Him, usually on a large, white, porcelain telephone.)

But such drinking—uh, *research*—tours at least provided us with fresh material. We developed so much material, in fact, that we had to delete a lot of beer games from our first book to get the nice, round, marketable number of 50.

These days, diplomas framed on our walls, we actually work for a living. College is a pleasant, fading memory; deadlines, mortgages, and layoffs are constant concerns. Many people, incidentally, have wondered how we convinced anyone to hire us. Look, creating the perfect résumé requires the same vivid imagination as creating a book on beer games. It's all a matter of writing a lot of nonsense and getting someone to buy it.

Anyway, upon entering the real world, we discovered something quite shocking: you can't research beer games until 3:00 a.m. and earn your pay at work the next day. In college, we could always bag classes and take a nap. But in the real world—brace yourselves—naps are very difficult to arrange.

Further, in college you could always act comatose, keep

You can always find other fun folks to regress with.

your mouth shut in class, and sleaze by. At work, people expect you to speak coherent sentences (often four or five at a time) and be productive and alert. These expectations rear their collective ugly head and tend to make you more, uh, responsible (the dreaded R-word).

That's the bad news. The good news is that most working people, when they get the chance (weekends, early evenings, holidays), act as immature as freshmen on a road trip. Don't you watch TV? We're living the Silver Bullet life! Who says you can't have pinstripes and rock 'n roll? Working hard all week makes you want to play hard all weekend. Friday nights are heavy duty, and you can always find other fun folks to regress with. Unless, that is, you make the mistake of becoming a lawyer. There are no fun lawyers. Anywhere.

The bottom line is, while we still have fun and play beer games and make idiots of ourselves on occasion, we don't have time for extensive research anymore. So, for this book, we relied heavily on those of you who graciously donated your ideas for new games to our world-famous Beer Research Department. Some of the games were excellent. Most of the grammar was not. But we're not complaining.

(By the way, since writing a letter involves considerable effort, careful thought, and finding a stamp, we are truly inspired by the number of letters we receive each week. Cheers to all who wrote—and to all who continue to write!)

Anyway, hoist those brew puppies while ye may, beer brothers and sisters. And drink a few for us.

FUN BEER FACT

Americans drink 6,991,000 12-ounce bottles (83,892,000 ounces; 656,406.25 gallons) of beer every hour.

A PLEA TO BEER DRINKERS EVERYWHERE

Perhaps the greatest thing about the USA (besides 24-hour convenience stores, of course) is the big D, Democracy. Yes, we the people—even we the beer-gaming people—can effect change and make our voices heard by those in power. The people cried out for relief from disco music; they demanded a change from Jimmy Carter; they became furious when Coca-Cola said it would change its recipe. And so the people got Bruce Springsteen, Ronald Reagan, and Classic Coke. The people were heard and obeyed! (On the other hand, the people also demanded Prohibition and Michael Bolton. Go figure.)

So, here's an opportunity for the beer-gaming people of the USA to rally behind two great causes:

CAUSE #1

We are always thrilled by the Olympic Games. But despite the brilliance of all the skiers, skaters, divers, runners, etc., there is something missing—**Blow Pong**. It's one of the classic sporting competitions (see our first book) of all time, and, since it's a Boot Factor 4 game, it remains an amateur event.

Blow Pong should be an Olympic sport! Imagine the possibilities if America fielded a Blow Pong team from, say, the University of Florida or Dartmouth. Gold medal city. Lobby the U.S. Olympic Committee by sending the card on the next page. You might also want to write the International Olympic Committee at Château de Vidy, CH-1007, Lausanne, Switzerland.

CAUSE #2

The authors should be guests on *The Late Show with David Letterman*. Their publisher tried to get them on when the first book came out, but no luck. But this time around, Dave must listen to the will of the people, and if you send him the card on the next page, he will have no choice but to yield to the forces of immaturity. Can you think of anything better than watching Dave play Beer Hunter? Neither can we. Write him today.

Dear U.S. Olympic Committee:

I urge you to make Blow Pong an Olympic sport. The game, which is described in **The Complete Book of Beer Drinking Games**, is a classic in the world of competition. Millions of beer drinkers around the globe would love to see the best amateur Blow Pong players compete. Plus, imagine how much more money you could make from beer commercials!

Name ....

Address ....

City .... State .... Zip ....

(From **Beer Games 2: The Exploitative Sequel** by Andy Griscom, Ben Rand, Scott Johnston, and Michael Balay. Published by Mustang Publishing, Memphis, TN.)

Dear Mr. Letterman:

I think the authors of **The Complete Book of Beer Drinking Games** and **Beer Games 2: The Exploitative Sequel** should be on your show. Since your show is the greatest talk show, and since they are the greatest beer gamers, it would be perfect. If you put them on, I promise to watch your show every night and to encourage others to watch it, too. I also promise to buy all the products advertised during the show. But if you don't put them on, we will harass CBS to replace you with Madonna.

Name ....

Address ....

City .... State .... Zip ....

(From **Beer Games 2: The Exploitative Sequel** by Andy Griscom, Ben Rand, Scott Johnston, and Michael Balay. Published by Mustang Publishing, Memphis, TN.)

MAIL TO:

U.S. Olympic Committee
One Olympic Plaza
Colorado Springs, CO 80909

MAIL TO:

Mr. David Letterman
"The Late Show"
CBS-TV
524 West 57th St.
New York, NY 10019

An Editorial
about Some Serious Shit

We deplore drunk driving. We've said that repeatedly, as forcefully as we can. Drunk drivers maim and kill thousands of people every year, and the loss to many families and communities is devastating. There are grounds for grave concern and judicious policy measures.

But our government has gone too far.

In the 1980's, the United States raised the drinking age to 21, as reason yielded to hysteria. Remember, the problem is not drinking *per se*. It's ludicrous to prevent college students from sharing a bottle of wine with their parents or to deny a young person a beer at a family picnic. It's downright un-American to keep a 20-year-old from having a cold beer after working the swing shift at the factory, especially since that same 20-year-old is old enough to enter into contracts, to sue and be sued, to vote, and, of course, to go to war.

Surely anyone old enough to get married is old enough to have a drink. God knows they'll need it. And what are the poor devils in Tennessee who get married at 14 supposed to do? Wait until they're 21 to have a bachelor party?

Seriously, is it fair to restrict the freedom of citizens simply because they belong to a certain age group? What if we proved that the vast majority of drunk drivers were age 33? Would we then forbid all 33-year-olds to drink? Right—you can drink from age 21 to 32, then you can't drink, then, when you turn 34, you can drink again. That's just as absurd as telling people they can't drink because they're 19.

We despise drunk drivers. But we believe that this issue has been abused and confused by certain bluenose groups who, deep down, really want to reinstate Prohibition.

Basically, these people want to impose their narrow-mind-

ed morality on everyone else, and the issue of college-age drinking was a convenient starting point. They have managed to foist their odious brand of Puritanism on the only group that lacks the money and the political muscle to fight back—the young.

You've probably seen lots of statistics marshaled to support these Neo-Prohibitionists. To these "facts," we offer two points. First, we agree with British prime minister Benjamin Disraeli, who said, "There are three kinds of lies in the world: lies, damned lies, and statistics." When the keepers of the statistics have an ax to grind, you can't expect illumination.

Second, causality is almost impossible to demonstrate in sociological phenomena. If the incidence of DUI falls when you raise the drinking age, can you really prove that a higher drinking age affected the DUI rate? Or could education, publicity, enforcement, and changing social and health trends have had an effect? Real life tends to be a lot more complicated than the bluenoses will admit.

Finally, of course, there's the inevitable question: Why is 21 such a magic number? Most drunk drivers are over 21. If raising the drinking age to 21 will prevent so many deaths, then raising it to 25, or 30, or 40 will prevent so many more!

Or perhaps age is irrelevant, and perhaps the key issue is **responsibility**. Funny, isn't it, how 18-year-olds are trusted with the greatest right in the world—the right to vote—but they're not responsible enough to drink a Bud. To pacify the screaming Neo-Prohibitionists, our political leaders found convenient scapegoats in people 18 to 20. "Those kids can't drink anymore, so that solves our drunk-driving problem." That's a lot easier than creating truly effective education programs, or really penalizing people who take no responsibility for their actions and drive while intoxicated.

We believe that it is fundamentally wrong to restrict any citizen's rights on the basis of his or her involuntary membership in a group. It is as wrong to prejudge an 18-year-old as irresponsible as it is to declare a person age 65 senile. It's called "discrimination," and it's contrary to everything America stands for.

However you look at it, the Neo-Prohibitionist arguments endorse age discrimination. They support paternalism and claim that they and the government know better than you.

We disagree. We believe that vigorous enforcement of stringent DUI laws and a graphic presentation of the dangers of drunk driving will convince any reasonable person that drunk driving is to be avoided and condemned. If you endanger yourself, that's your business and, indeed, your right. But endangering other people is way out of line.

College-age drinking is **not** synonymous with drunk driving. Period. Instead of wasting the resources of our over-burdened legal system on drinkers under 21, politicians and "concerned citizens" should be educating all drivers and enforcing current laws. Meanwhile, as the Neo-Prohibitionists and the lawmakers sweat about fraternity houses having keg parties with 20-year-olds present, thousands are still dying on the roads every year.

Beer Game Etiquette

To tell you the truth, beer game etiquette is a contradiction in terms. Beer games are often rude, and players even ruder. In an attempt to curb gross incivility, an altogether arbitrary set of rules has evolved among veteran gamesters.

Well, that's not really honest. The truth is, the more rules players must remember, the more infractions they make, and the more beer they drink. And this, after all, is the whole idea.

Beer game etiquette varies from one geopolitical region to another—indeed, from one game to another. There are, however, ten common rules players may invoke:

RULE 1

No Pointing. Since pointing is one of the most frequent acts, especially when identifying players who blunder, there naturally must be a rule against it. Anyone who points with his finger must take a swig from his beer. The only acceptable way to point is with a bent elbow.*

Gamesters may use only their elbows to point.

RULE 2

No Saying the Word "Drink." Whenever players use the word "drink" in any form (e.g., drinking, drinkable, drunk, drank, drinked, drinkly, etc.), they must drink—er, imbibe.

---

*This practice originated with the game Whales Tails. Since whales don't have fingers, they must point with a flipper, assuming they want to point at something. When a human points with his elbow, it resembles a whale pointing with his flipper. Sort of.

Be sure to read "Beer Game Etiquette" to all players before you begin an evening of gaming.

Wrong Hands. Right-handed players are forbidden to drink with their right hands, and left-handed players with their left. For the hard core, there is no drinking with either hand. When players infringe, they must drink again. Incidentally, it's poor sportsmanship to sit on your drinking hand or zip it inside your pants.

No Profanity. This needs no explanation, but it will drive you apeshit.

The Ten Minute Warning. In addition to Rule #1, this is considered a standard regulation. Players must give a ten minute warning before quitting a beer game. This prevents a player who just lost big-time from shirking his penalties by claiming he hears his mother calling and dashing off, leaving the three pitchers he was supposed to chug.

No Pronouns. This is one of the most difficult rules. By excluding pronouns, players get confused when they try to identify each other. This makes them point, and so they violate Rule #1, and so they drink.

 First Infraction. If a player makes a mistake and the game continues for a while before players realize the infraction, any blunders after the original are nullified. Void where prohibited by law.

Discreet Digit. During a game, a player can discreetly hang his forefinger off the edge of the table. Players who see this quietly do the same as they continue to play the game. The last player to hang a digit drinks.

 Golden Chair. Before a player leaves the game to go to the bathroom for a visit with Captain Leaky or for a casual reverse drink, he must say, "Golden chair" to gain immunity from being called while absent. This rule is crucial in verbal tag games in which players away on "business" often get called mistakenly.

Point of Order. Unless you are in the 8th grade (a.k.a. "the best two years of our lives"), you will rarely have parents around to supervise your beer games and make impartial rulings. So, the Point of Order establishes a tribunal to settle arguments, clarify rules, and make additions to a game. When a problem arises, a player should yell, "Point of order!" All players raise their elbows into the air and yell in response, "Point of order!" They then put their fists in the middle of the table with their thumbs sticking out sideways. The player who initiated the Point of Order states what the players are voting on—to introduce a new rule, for example, or determine whether Rufus may go to the bathroom. He then yells, "Vote!" and the players point their thumbs up for approval or down for denial. A denied motion must be accompanied by a loud buzzing sound by the whole tribunal, just like when the fat lady loses on *The Price Is Right*.

The Social Drink Rule ensures fun for the whole group.

Note: *The rules below were created by readers and sent to the Beer Research Department.*

RULE 11

The Social Drink. A great way to increase the Boot Factor of low-rated games, a "social" requires everyone to drink when a pre-determined event occurs. Call for a social whenever anyone rolls double 6's in a dice game, for example, or gets the ace of spades in a card game. It's also the only way to make sure that expert gamesters drink at least something.

RULE 12

Name Your God. Many beer games require the presence of an impartial person to announce the rules, start contests, make judgment calls, etc. At the beginning of such games, players should name a "God," who has total power and must be obeyed completely. The Point of Order tribunal can penalize any player showing disrespect for God.

Joaning. Before they play beer games, the Crockers of Ballwin, MO warm up with "joaning"—known elsewhere as "snapping" or "playing the dozens." It's basically trading witty insults, such as "You're so stupid that you tried to put M&M's in alphabetical order," or "You're so ugly that when you were born, the doctor slapped your mother." Such banter can continue throughout the evening, and players who get "joaned" so badly that they can't respond must drink a full brew.

Reverse Cap. This rule states that gamesters must wear baseball caps when they begin play. When the player is buzzed, he must turn his cap around backwards. If he forgets to do so and the other players decide he's toxxed, then he must pound a brew.

Mega-Courtesy. Developed by Russ Haynal and his frat brothers in Troy, NY, Mega-Courtesy can make a typical debauched beer game seem like High Tea with the Queen. When this rule is invoked, players must adopt a British accent and be exceedingly polite. Anyone failing the ultra-strict standards of Mega-Courtesy must imbibe. For example, if a player is gloating over another's misfortune, a gamester can say, "I don't think that's very nice of you," and the gloating player must respond, "Yes, I'm sorry, I'll drink right now." Or, if you yourself punish a player severely (e.g., you sink five straight quarters), you should say, "I'm sorry for making you drink five straight times. I'll chug to apologize." But remember, as Russ said, "Players don't try to catch each other infringing on Mega-Courtesy because that would be, well, not courteous." He also wrote, "Making any game a courteous one is guaranteed to double or triple the alcohol consumption." As a matter of courtesy, we've warned you.

THE BEER BONG

Many readers have asked if we have heard of a "beer bong," and, if so, how come we didn't describe it in our first book. Silly mortals. Of course, we—Beer Gods, remember?—have heard of beer bongs. We've also seen them, touched them, used them, and even built one or two.

So why didn't we write about them? Simple—we don't much like them.

Look, we don't drink beer only to get blitzed, though that's a pleasant side effect. If we only wanted to get drunk, we could do about six shots of Jägermeister and, *voila!*, Blitzberg.

No, we drink beer because we *love beer.* We love the taste, the color, the carbonation, the variety, the social aspects, etc. With a beer bong, you don't even taste the beer. Two or three beevos can shoot down your throat in a few seconds, and all you've got to show for it is a swollen gut. What's the point?

Sure, beer bongs are fun to try once or twice. So here's how to make one: Get a large plastic funnel (8-12 inches) and about two feet of plastic tube. Attach the funnel to one end of the tube with a hose clamp. That's it.

Here's how to use one: Keep the open end of the tube level with the top of the funnel and pour as much beer as you can (usually over 30 ounces) into the funnel. Exhale, place your mouth over the open end of the tube, raise the funnel as high as you can, and drop to one knee. The beer will rifle down your throat incredibly fast. Macho drinkers blow the excess foam through the funnel and then emit a sonic belch.

Try it once so you can say, "Been there. Done that." Then enjoy your beer one at a time, the way we do.

The Boot Factor

(a.k.a. Earl Indicator, Ralph Rating, Vomit Vector)

The Boot Factor, using a scale of one to five, indicates the level of havoc a beer game will wreak upon your digestive system. The Boot Factor rates a game's capacity to stimulate a little-known area in the brain, the *regurgitus violentus loci*. A Boot Factor of 1 describes the lowest potential for tossing cookies, while a Boot Factor of 5 warns of an almost assured heave.*

However, the Boot Factor is more than just a guideline. Used wisely, it can provide essential pre-game information that you should use to plot strategy. For example, in a game with a low Boot Factor, concentrate on ways to defeat fellow players by using your intellect, such as it is. But after a few rounds of a high-Factor game, very little intellect remains, so players must focus on immediate physical concerns ("How big is my stomach?") and reserve thoughts on strategy for less cerebral matters ("Where is the closest toilet?").

For over-achievers, the Boot Factor provides a numerical incentive for consuming massive quantities of brew. Tell your bookworm friend that the Boot Factor can be compared to his G.P.A., with 5 being the *summa cum laude* of beer gaming. The knowledge that you are a regular upper-level competitor can do wonders for your self-esteem, not to mention attract countless fawning members of the opposite sex.

Use the Boot Factor strictly for comparison. Volume and frequency of gastrointestinal evacuations may vary with length of game and size of penalty. Your actual game mileage may be less. See dealer for complete details.

BOOT FACTOR ONE

Games rated **Boot Factor One** serve as an introduction for the neophyte in quest of the upper echelons of beer gaming. For experienced players, Boot Factor One games can serve as limbering exercises for the more demanding contests to follow. Since this book is a sequel, however, we believe its readers will be too advanced for Boot Factor One games, so no B.F. 1 games are included in this book.

BOOT FACTOR TWO

The **Boot Factor Two games** teach fundamental principles of beer gaming while still boasting a low regurgitation potential. With these contests, the gamester can acquire and hone the skills that earn survival in most upper-level games: mastering the unique verbal and non-verbal language associated with beer gaming, knowing whom *not* to sit next to (lightweights are always the first to york), and training your bladder to retain many more ounces of fluid than it has ever held before.

Wisconsin Air Slams	Beer 99 Revisited
Bolender Ball	Jacuzzi Ball
Bobbing for Beer	Drink It
Mine Field	Spoons

Wisconsin Air Slams

Boot Factor: 2

We like this game, sent to us by Brian Griesbach at the Univ. of Wisconsin in Madison, because it embraces the spirit of witless abandon we encourage. Also, we like it because the rules can be written on a matchbook—with room to spare.

First, find a place where the beer is free. Since you should always be on the lookout for such places, this shouldn't pose a problem. (However, never play inside your own house, unless you enjoy watching real estate be condemned.)

Second, fill a plastic cup with beer.

Finally, throw the cup high over your head and drink all the beer you can as it falls to the ground.

You can play **Wisconsin Air Slams** one-on-one and take turns, or in teams and toss the beer to your partner. You can also play in large groups, which could be a lot of fun in, say, Daytona Beach during Spring Break. You could even play by yourself, but don't try it within sight of a mental institution.

Honor and glory goes to the first player buzzed, the player who tosses the cup highest, the wettest player, the driest player, and any reader who believes that anyone ever really plays this game.

**"Man, being reasonable, must get drunk.
The best of life is but intoxication."
Lord Byron, *Don Juan***

Bolender Ball

Boot Factor: 2

Bolender Ball is named for a legendary literary figure, Mark "Eat Me" Bolender, who was renowned for his utter ineptitude at **Bolender Ball**, which, before we named it after him, was called simply "the ricochet-the-ball-off-the-other-guy's-face" game.

To play, assemble a group of four or more happy gamesters in a circle and produce a ball of some sort. Purists favor old, lopsided footballs, but softballs, medicine balls, or, if the players are especially vicious, golf balls will be fine. Beach balls are no good, and bowling balls are okay only if your gaming partners include Mount Rushmore.

The object of **Bolender Ball** is to toss the ball at close range among players until someone drops it. Mr. Butterfingers then drinks. Under actual game conditions, players quickly realize

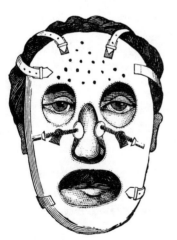

that the best way to make an opponent drop the ball is to hurl it mightily at his face when he least expects it. After that discovery, **Bolender Ball** becomes quite interesting and especially manly.

Ideally, you should play the game in a small room with many windows and other breakables, which add to the atmosphere of anarchy and naked fear. A liberal display of open beer bottles perched precariously on the edges of tables is also key.

Our only advice to players is this: cover your crotch, and never play in your own room.

A Bolender Ball *wuss.*

Bobbing for Beer

Boot Factor: 2

Have you ever faced that time at a party when there's a lull and you know that if things don't pick up immediately, the festivities will die? People are long past **Bullshit** or **Thumper**, but it's too early for **Kill the Keg**. So how do you jump-start the action?

Timothy White of Metamora, MI has the answer. He wrote that he and his fraternity brothers like to instigate a round of **Bobbing for Beer**. They get a plastic, industrial-size garbage can, put a large number of beer bottles in the bottom, and fill the can with ice and water. They then get volunteers (or hapless pledges), make them put their hands in their pockets, turn them upside down, and dunk them in the can for five to ten seconds. The dunker must surface with a bottle in his mouth. If he succeeds, he can make someone chug. If not, he must chug—and keep getting dunked until he succeeds.

A great crowd-pleaser, **Bobbing for Beer** is guaranteed to get any party back on track. And, Tim says, "especially when females do it, it's an uplifting experience."

Eight More Synonyms for Beer

cold smiles	liquid protein
ha-ha's	medicine
plasma	gold chowder
fun juice	lava

Mine Field

Boot Factor: 2

Mine Field and the game on page 39, **Jacuzzi Ball**, complete our portfolio of aquatic beer games. (ESPN once interviewed us because they saw a video of Ben performing a stupendous aqua-boot.) Our thanks to Doug Krause of Harlingen, TX for sending this game to us.

To play **Mine Field**, an impartial, non-playing person must fill a number of empty beer cans with water and toss them throughout a swimming pool. (Players can't watch while the "mines" are laid, by the way.) Then the "miner" should shake up a full can of beer and toss it into the pool as well.

Players then dive into the pool and try to find the shaken can. Whoever locates the "live mine" has the distinct privilege of opening it under the nose of any player he chooses. That unlucky gamester gets his nostrils washed, and he must chug the rest of the beer in the can.

One note for all water-based beer games: players who commit an aqua-boot display very bad etiquette and must sit in a corner with the bug-skimming net over their heads.

Beer 99 Revisited

Boot Factor: 2

When we reviewed our description of **Beer 99** in our first book, we realized that our entry was inadequate. In particular, we neglected to illuminate some of the finer points of strategy (i.e., "cheating") familiar to accomplished **Beer 99** players. The following is our effort to remedy that oversight.

A Brief Review of the Game

Beer 99 is a card game in which deception and sleazy tactics mean success, and honesty means failure. Each player receives four cards, which he should conceal from fellow players. The value of a card is the same as in blackjack (aces are one or eleven; face cards are ten). The first player throws one card face up onto the discard pile and announces the value of his card. The next player also throws one card onto the pile and announces the sum of his card plus the first card.

The game continues in this fashion, with each player adding his card's value to the total. If the pile totals 99, then the player next in rotation must drink. But if a player sends the value over 99, then he must drink. When 99 is reached, the cards are shuffled, and the pile's value starts over at zero.

There are several ways to avoid going over 99. Kings, 10's, and 4's all have special properties. A king can give the total of 99 to anyone the player chooses. A 10 can either raise or lower the value by ten, so someone who gets 99 can play a 10 and announce 89 to avoid drinking. A 4 lets you skip a turn.

Also, a player must drink if he has no cards left when it becomes his turn to discard. To keep a full hand, players should always draw a new card after discarding. But the only time you're permitted to draw is immediately after discarding, so you must stay alert.

The Finer Points of Play

Now a few words about cheating, which is where most of the fun and skill come into **Beer 99**. A good player will always have a supply of cards in hand, shoe, sleeve, sock, etc. Deft players can pilfer two or three cards at a time from the pile or from other players. The possibilities are endless, but here are a few tried-and-true tactics:

The Mass Grab: This famous technique works best in a crowded, noisy room. The Mass Grabber seizes up to half a deck when he draws, on the theory that it will increase his chance of getting a strong hand.

The Elvis Defense: Use this tactic when the count is 99 and you can't defend yourself. You simply shout, "Look! It's Elvis!"or maybe, "My God! Nikki is taking her shirt off!" while pointing to the far corner of the room. In the ensuing uproar, grab some cards from the deck. Be advised that this dramatic maneuver works only once or twice per evening.

The Miscount: This tactic relies mainly on your opponents' incompetence. Simply play a card and announce the wrong total. For example, suppose the count is 99 and you're defenseless. Just play an 8 and calmly declare, "90." Remember, there is no correlation between what you have in your hand and what you can get away with.

The Instant Replay: This ruse works best while Nikki is putting her shirt back on. Just pick up the last card played, and play it again. Extra style points go to the stud who can pick up the king just played, look at the player who just played it right in the eye, and announce, "99 to *you!*"

The Quick Pick: Not much skill here, but you'll need *cajones* the size of cantaloupes. Take cards from the deck *before* you play your card. If you like the card you've drawn, play it; if not, just keep drawing. Investment bankers and used-car salesmen are great at this maneuver.

The Misdeal: We really like this tactic because it demonstrates real sleaze, as well as clever foresight. You're the dealer, so you deal too many cards to one player. Wait until things get tight for you, then accuse your victim of cheating. Whoops! The whole hand must be scrapped, and the lowlife "cheater" must drink. Brilliant.

A Final Caution

Remember, although cheating is an integral part of **Beer 99**, it is **not** legal, and cheaters who get caught must face the consequences. If a player is accused of cheating, all players must vote on his guilt or innocence by showing "thumbs up" or "thumbs down." If the majority votes guilty, the scoundrel must drink.

So you see, **Beer 99** is a lot like life: have fun, but don't get caught.

Just a Test

Our publisher is a hosehead.
Our publisher is a hosehead.
Our publisher is a hosehead.

We just wanted to see if we could sneak this in.
Thank you for your cooperation.

Jacuzzi Ball

Boot Factor: 2

Legend has it that **Jacuzzi Ball** originated in Aspen, skiing's answer to Daytona Beach. Those who like to combine beer-gaming with more, er, adult pursuits will love this game.

The premise of **Jacuzzi Ball** is quite simple. Find a Jacuzzi, fill it with six or more people, and place an empty can of beer in the water. The object of the game: avoid being touched by the beer as it bobs and swirls around. Whoever touches it drinks it.

The clever of you out there in Readerland will quickly realize that moving rapidly in a small Jacuzzi filled with bodies trying also to move rapidly is no easy task—though it can be easy to enjoy. Players tend to bump into each other, and the more they drink, the more they bump. Hence, you should strive for an advantageous number of men and women in the pool,* as scantily clad as negotiations will allow.

Jacuzzi Ball makes an excellent competitive sport, too. Put a wrestler, a defensive lineman, a hockey player, and a rugby player in the same tub, and tell them anything goes. Then stand back—quickly—and take bets. (Of course, never use bottles for competition **Jacuzzi Ball**.)

If you find yourself short of players, or if you just want to drink more, you can always add more cans. Ping-Pong balls also work well.

A popular variation is **Strip Jacuzzi Ball** (SJB). If the can touches you, you must drink *and* remove a piece of clothing. Obviously, this will be a brief game if the players wear one-piece bathing suits, so gamesters should dress elaborately—formal evening wear is especially sporting—before entering the tub.

One male per six females is ideal, in our experience.

Drink It *was your goofy uncle's favorite party game.*

Drink It

Boot Factor: 2

"Randee," from Carson City, NV, sent us the most inane, witless, pointless, nonsensical, moronic, utterly idiotic beer game that's ever been sent to the Beer Research Department.

We wish we'd created it.

To play **Drink It**, simply ask someone a question that can be answered with one or two words, such as "What's your favorite football team?" When they say, "Vikings," you exclaim, "Then drink it!" That person then must take seven swallows of beer—one for every letter in the answer—as you spell out the word.

If Beavis and Butt-head could drink beer, this is the game they'd play. Over and over and over.

Of course, there's limitless potential for abuse here, especially when you know how the person will answer. Ask a good friend where he's from; he'll look at you like you're an idiot and say, "Chattanooga, Tennessee." And you can guffaw loudly as you reply, "Then drink it!"

We should note one drawback to this game. Experienced **Drink It** players tend to get paranoid and start to limit their vocabulary to words under four letters or primitive grunts. Often, however, no one notices any difference.

Drink It has a low Boot Factor because most people will only answer two or three questions before they walk away from you muttering, "Man, that's the dumbest game of all time." The Beavis and Butt-head version, however, would make it a solid B.F. 5.

Randee, oh Randee! **Drink It** is ingenious: a simple but sociable challenge, a hearty laugh, a chance for mass consumption. With one hastily written missive, you hit the primordial core of beer gaming, while we bumbling scribes have used thousands of words and dozens of pages to try to describe the ethos of this activity. We stand in awe, Beer Goddess, and we beg you to send us your picture.

Spoons

Boot Factor: 2

Spoons is not, as drug subculturists may hope, a game played with a powdery, white derivative of the coca plant. Nor does it involve the sophomoric practice of spooning beer from a soup bowl to increase its buzz potential. No, **Spoons** is a legal beer game for mature beer gamers (yes, that is contradictory).

To play **Spoons**, you need only three things: cards, beer, and those ever-popular kitchen utensils, spoons. This is a great game for a rainy Sunday afternoon. Or play right after dessert, when the equipment is warmed up and accessible.

In the middle of a table, place one less spoon than players (i.e., if you have six players, use five spoons). The more players, the better, and be sure everyone has an equal reach for the spoons.

The dealer begins by giving each player four cards. The object is to get four of a kind, and, since it's unlikely anyone will be dealt this, the dealer must examine his cards, draw a new card from the deck, and pass one card to his right. The next player also passes a card to his right, and so on. When it's the dealer's turn again, he should draw a new card and repeat the procedure. Whoever gets four of a kind should immediately shout, "Spoons!" and grab a spoon from the pile. At that point, everyone else may also grab a spoon, and the sap left spoonless must chug a beer.

Note #1: It's perfectly legal to attempt a "fake grab" for a spoon by yelling "Tunes!" or

"Rooms!" or something and smacking your hand near the pile, hoping to entrap some over-eager spoonmonger.

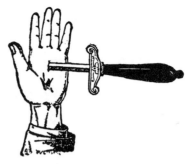

This is why we play Spoons, not Knives.

Note #2: There is no such thing as a personal foul, so you can imagine that **Spoons** can get rowdy. You can also see why we strongly discourage you from substituting other popular utensils— namely, knives and forks— for spoons. Your vital organs (except perhaps your liver) will thank us.

The Ten Stages of Drunkenness

1. Witty & Charming
2. Rich & Powerful
3. Benevolent
4. I Can Dance
5. Clairvoyant
6. Screw Dinner
7. Patriotic
8. Witty & Charming, Part II
9. Invisible
10. Bulletproof

Thanks to Sue Christopherson & Al Wharton from Nashville, TN for sending this to the Beer Research Dept.

Chugging with Ivan, Circa 1984:
A True Story

By: Someone Who Knows

"**Beer is not popular** in my country," said Andrei Souvorov, Second Secretary of the Soviet Mission to the United Nations.

"*Say what?!*" I replied, incredulous.

"We prefer *wodka*, my Americanski friend. Here, have some more Stolichnaya."

Well, I thought, it's not a bad offer. After all, I wasn't paying. But there was still a big problem with this party, other than the two-way mirrors and the stiff, unsmiling men talking into their cuff links—no brew! There wasn't a stray frosty anywhere in the Soviet consulate, and I was getting desperate.

So my friends and I suggested a better idea. We asked our new Communist chums if they would like to blow their lavish joint and join us in the great American custom of drinking beer in a dive bar.

After a moment of collective reflection, they agreed. Heck, they *already* knew how to drink too much and slap each other on the back. All they had to do was switch from vodka to beer. So off we marched, leaving the consulate and heading straight for an Irish dive.

We made a most unlikely crew: the Second and Third Secretaries of the Soviet Mission, the chief correspondent for Moscow television in New York, and three fire-breathing, free enterprise-loving capitalists. We had learned earlier that at least two of our new comrades probably were KGB. Of course, we found that quite amusing. We would be careful not to reveal any classified beer game secrets.

Once at the bar, we handily polished off pitcher after pitcher and tried to teach our new friends some classic American drinking games. However, we found that the best sport was backing the Soviets into logical corners. ("And speaking of New York fashion models, Andrei, how is it exactly that the workers' revolution never came to America?") This was even more fun than delivering the death blow in U Chug.

Almost as enjoyable was listening to Andrei's interpretation of current events. "You cannot tell me you have economic recovery in the United States," he said. "This is only the work of your propagandists in Washington. All but the richest Americans are poor and oppressed, and their children are forced to work at McDonald's so your President can build more nuclear bombs. I know of these things."

"I'm sure you do," I said. "Have another beer and maybe you'll see things more clearly."

"I can hardly see at all, my American friend!" he said laughing. "It is time I and my comrades returned to the consulate."

"Okay," I said, "but you pay. That's another great American tradition—he who leaves first must pay."

Not being one to break traditions, Andrei agreed. And I, thinking that in some way $50 had been diverted from purchasing torture equipment for a gulag in Siberia, was pretty pleased. That is, until I saw Andrei whip out his American Express card.

"You don't know me, but I have forced economic deprivation and cultural stagnation on billions of people worldwide. That's why I never leave Moscow without..."

It seems I had only managed to divert $50 from Bloomingdale's.

"Goodnight, my new American friend," Andrei said. "Let me say that I do not agree with what you say on politics, but I very much enjoy these Dunk the Duchess and Boot-a-Bout games you have taught us to play. I cannot wait to share these with my comrades in Moscow! Perhaps, my friend, if we had more such fun times between your countrymen and mine, much of the tension between our people today would be gone."

Yes, and so would much of the world's strategic beer reserves, but that's another story.

So my friends and I left the Irish dive with the hope that maybe, just maybe, we had accomplished something really important that evening.

Chugging with Ivan: It was one small gulp for a man, and one giant chug for international depravity.

Publisher's Note: Communism and the Soviet Union collapsed a few years after the fateful night described above. Coincidence? We don't think so. We say, it wasn't George Bush who ended the Cold War; it was Anheuser-Busch.

BOOT FACTOR THREE

Penalties in **Boot Factor Three** games are generally no more stringent than those in Boot Factor Two. However, since they require more mental and physical agility, Boot Factor Three games are more difficult to play. At this level, players tend to falter more often and therefore drink more frequently. But violent heaves are still uncommon, although players will sometimes opt for the self-induced ralph (a.k.a. "bootlimia") to mollify the next morning's hangover.

Suck and Blow
Dice of Death
Quarters Variations
Sink the Cap
Bombardier
Dissociation
Squat
Stores

Suck and Blow

Boot Factor: 3

As the shrewd beer gamester might surmise, **Suck and Blow** ranks high on the list of coed beer games. The contest itself is a simple test of oral dexterity, but it can lead to much more complicated things. Like marriage.

As Leslie Thomas of Auburn, NE explained to us, the game requires at least six players sitting in a circle, plus a deck of cards. Players attempt to pass a card around the circle using only their mouths. The card is affixed to a player's mouth and held in place by suction. This player must pass the card to the next player by blowing on the card while the other player sucks on it. Naturally, the closer the mouths, the easier the

pass. If the card is dropped, both passer and receiver must drink.

If you haven't guessed by now that players should sit boy-girl-boy-girl, then you're reading the wrong book.

A few hints on strategy: Your tongue can be very helpful in this game, not because it helps you pass the card, but because if you drop the card in mid-pass, your tongue could end up in some very interesting places. So even if you drop the card, you can often claim a victory of sorts. Also, remember to brush your teeth before the game, and throw away that slimy deck of cards afterwards.

Dice of Death

Boot Factor: 3

In the most auspicious debut of any beer game in years, **Dice of Death** was pioneered at the beach one chilly spring day.

Originally a Navy contest called "Ship, Captain, and Crew," this game was used by midshipmen to see who would buy the next round. The Navy version is interminably dull, however, and only people who love long sea voyages with lots of guys with crew cuts would enjoy it.

Not to worry, though. By the time we refined (and renamed) it, **Dice of Death** was ready for the pantheon of beer game classics, and we were ready for another pantheon entirely.

The object of the game is to avoid being the last player to roll double sixes. If you are, you must roll the dice to determine how many shots of beer you must drink. Getting a 12 on this roll is known as rolling the "boxcars of doom."

Perhaps this sounds a bit boring? Well, there's more:

If you roll:	*Then you must:*
a 2 or 3	drink one shot
double 2's, 3's, 4's, or 5's	make anyone drink one shot
one die off the table	drink one shot
two dice off the table	drink two shots
one die within a thumb's length of the edge	make anyone drink one shot
two dice within a thumb's length of the edge	make two people drink one shot, or one person drink two shots
the dice into the cup (on one bounce)	everyone else drinks one shot if you sink one die, two shots if you sink both.

To obtain the best bouncing action, a formica or glass table is key.

Dice of Death is a thrilling, action-packed game. The excitement on the last roll is awesome, and the ability to screw other people is always amusing. As with all our beer games, feel free to innovate.

Ten Things Guys Think about When Drinking Beer

1. unhealthy food
2. loud music
3. loose women
4. Captain Leaky
5. sleep
6. Anna Nicole Smith
7. football
8. capitalism (*as in "Gee, it's great"*)
9. fatalism as a philosophical fallacy
10. more beer

Quarters Variations

Boot Factor: 3

We were hesitant to describe all the variations on **Quarters** that readers sent to the Beer Research Department. After baseball, **Quarters** is the most popular religion in America. For us—the official chroniclers of the game—to disseminate such heterodox concepts would be unseemly, we thought. It would be like introducing the designated hitter, artificial turf, and nighttime World Series games all in the same week—no circle of the Inferno is deep enough to punish such a crime. The game is the thing.

In its pure, unadulterated form, **Quarters** is the essence of powerful simplicity, like the curves on Elle Macpherson. You have the cup, bright with slowly bubbling beer. You have the table, dark and scarred wood in the dark and scarred bar, where the beer is cheap and the women are brave. You have the quarter, gleaming, cold and wet in your clammy palm. You have the delicious tension of hope mingled with anxiety: *Will Rodney sink it again? Will he make Moose drink for the 17th straight time? Will Moose tear out Rodney's eyes and piss on his brain?* You have the carefully measured approach before the shot, the floating arc of the toss, the solid rebound, the musical plink of metal into beery waves, the cries of triumph and despair, and finally, most beautifully, the sound of Moose saying, "Shit, I swallowed the quarter."

But we realize that we have a responsibility to numerous readers

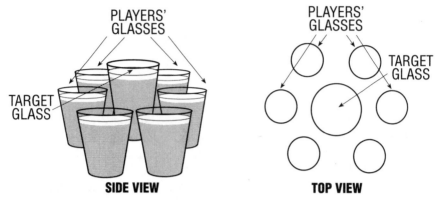

PLAYERS' GLASSES	PLAYERS' GLASSES
TARGET GLASS	TARGET GLASS
SIDE VIEW	**TOP VIEW**

Chandeliers for Six Players

who wrote to us with their variations on the traditional game. Three mutations of **Quarters** are especially notable:

Chandeliers

Chandeliers, also known as **Carousel Quarters**, is a method of enhancing the drinking opportunities in **Quarters** for those players too uncoordinated to master the classic version of the game. The kind of person who prefers six wild cards in poker over straight five-card stud will enjoy **Chandeliers**.

To play, simply arrange one glass for each player in a circle around a target glass. Each player is assigned the glass nearest him. If you bounce the quarter into someone else's glass, he drinks, and you may throw again. If you bounce it into the center glass, you can make anyone drink. If you bounce it into your own glass, you are a complete hosehead. You drink and forfeit your turn.

We can't imagine why you would want to play **Chandeliers** over straight **Quarters**. That is, unless you think it will reduce your chances of catching the latest sexual virus. Fear not. As of this writing, drinking beer out of someone else's glass is not considered a "high-risk sexual activity."

Suicide Quarters

This manly variation of **Quarters** requires two glasses; place the second glass directly behind the first (from the perspective of the thrower). If the quarter lands in the first glass, you can make anyone drink. However, if you propel the coin into the second glass, you must drink both beers and lose your turn.

Hey, we warned you it was manly.

The Dartmouth Double

A recent road trip to Dartmouth for a football weekend renewed our faith in American youth. We arrived on campus and followed our noses to the nearest fraternity party. When we say we "followed our noses," we don't mean that we used our well-developed instinct for finding festivity. Rather, we just searched for the source of a uniquely nauseous odor (sort of a combination of antique regurgitation, Pine-Sol, and academic probation) that permeated the frat houses.

The stench, we discovered, wafted from a basement, where we found American youth at play. What they played was **Quarters**, and they played it so well that we doubted their claim of amateur status. Luckily for us all, they had created a **Quarters** variation to bring them back to the level of mortals.

The Dartmouth gamesters play with two quarters at the same time, and, of course, two cups of beer as targets. The game progresses according to the traditional rules until both quarters land in one player's hands. At this point, the player must bounce both the quarters simultaneously.

If you're not ambidextrous, you can forget about sinking either coin. The **Dartmouth Double** prevents excessively long runs by one talented player and consequently prevents excessive drunkenness before, say, 8:00 p.m. After you miss both shots, it is good form to "double" on one quarter and pass the other coin to another player.

After playing this game, we decided there may be a place for constructive change, even in something as basic as the rules to the Grand Old Game.

15 Reasons Why Beer Is Better than Women

1. You can enjoy a beer all month long.
2. You don't have to wine and dine beer.
3. Your beer will always wait patiently for you in the car while you play golf.
4. Beer is never late.
5. Hangovers go away.
6. A beer doesn't get jealous when you grab another beer.
7. Beer tops come off with little effort.
8. When you go to a bar, you can always pick up a beer.
9. Beer never has a headache.
10. A beer won't get upset if you come home with beer on your breath.
11. If you pour a beer right, you always get good head.
12. You can have more than one beer a night and not feel guilty.
13. You can share a beer with your friends.
14. You can have a beer in public.
15. Most beer is better when it's frigid.

Sink the Cap

Boot Factor: 3

One of the most popular games in our first book was **Dunk the Duchess**. In the many letters we've received from readers, we've learned a few things about that game. First, **Dunk the Duchess** is also known as "Sink the Titanic" and "Piss in the Bucket," depending on where you're from and whether you graduated from high school.

Second, according to Philip Dendy of Security, CO, there's a game played in the Rockies called **Sink the Cap**. It's a lot like **Dunk the Duchess**, but it can be played even when pitchers aren't handy, should you ever be in such desperate straits. Essentially, the rules are the same for both games, but in **Sink the Cap**, a glass substitutes for the pitcher, and a bottle cap takes the place of the glass.

To play, fill a glass with beer, eliminate the foam, and float a bottle cap on the surface of the beer. Take turns pouring beer into the cap. Whoever sinks the cap must drink the whole cup.

By the way, resting your beer on the side of the glass while pouring is considered horribly inconsiderate and schmo-like, so don't do it.

"Beer is not a good cocktail-party drink, especially in a home where you don't know where the bathroom is."
Billy Carter

Bombardier

Boot Factor: 3

Bombardier was inspired by a trip to one of those huge, suburban movie theaters (you know, the ones with names like "Cinema 1-n"). In the lobby, a charity was soliciting money with a clever gimmick: moviegoers could try to win free admission by dropping a quarter into a small glass at the bottom of a large tank of water. Of course, it's pure luck if you win, since the quarter darts through the water at totally unpredictable angles.

Two good things came of this: the charity raised a lot of money, and we invented a new beer game.

Instead of a large tank and a glass, **Bombardier** requires a pitcher of beer and a shot glass. Players take turns dropping dimes (quarters are too big) into the pitcher, trying to get them to land in the shot glass. To ensure that the shot is tough, players must place their elbows on top of the pitcher and drop the dime from that height.

If you don't get the dime in the glass, you drink (directly from the pitcher, stud). If you do sink the dime, everyone else must go see a movie. No, no—just kidding. Everyone else must drink, of course (from another pitcher, preferably). If you are an utter chucklehead and totally miss the pitcher—it's happened, believe us—you must kill the *entire* pitcher.

Of course, there will be less and less beer in the pitcher as the game progresses, so getting the dime in the glass will become easier. Therefore (math majors take note), the amount of drinking will increase in direct proportion to the inverse of the square of the amount of beer left in the pitcher.

That is,

$$SOI = 1/BIP^2,$$

where SOI=State of Inebriation and BIP=Beer in Pitcher. And, since SOI=OOP (Odds of Puking), then it's obvious that

$$OOP = 1/BIP^2.$$

This is known as the **Transitive Property of Booting** (TPB).
Of course, when the pitcher is empty, collect all the dimes and buy the next round. Bombs away!

Dissociation

Boot Factor: 3

This game proves that beer makes your thoughts clearer, more rational, more connected, and better defined. Simply, **Dissociation** is one of the toughest beer games ever.

Players sit around a keg or a pitcher, and one player volunteers to go first, if he knows what's good for him. This savvy gamester begins by saying any word or phrase. It can be "The 1968 Rose Bowl," or "Counselor Troi's cleavage," or "boiled crawfish," or "The Amazing Mr. Lifto."

Proceeding clockwise, the next player must name something that has **no connection whatsoever** with the word or phrase previously stated, and the other players judge whether there is any link. It may be dubious; it may be tenuous; it may be within the wildest flights of imagination—but if there's any connection at all, the player who fails to dissociate must drink.

Some examples: If the first player says, "final exams," and you say, "keg of beer," you must chug, because drinking a keg of beer is what most normal students do when they should be studying for final exams. Or suppose a worthless English-major-type says "Proust," and you respond with "Chicken Mc-Nuggets." You drink, because Chicken McNuggets are made of chicken (we think), and Frank Perdue sells chickens, and Proust wrote a book called *A la Recherche du Temps Perdu* ("A Remembrance of the Times of Perdu"). On the other hand, if you answer "Baudelaire," you'll go scot-free, if your friends are anything like ours. That's stretching it, of course, but that's why this game is such a monster.

Two tips: Never answer with the words "beer," "sex," and "food," because they are (or should be) connected to everything. And never play with lawyers.

As the night goes on, you will become shocked at how your mind will not dissociate and how everything seems to lead to everything else. Your thoughts become connected to the words and thoughts of your fellow players, no matter how hard you resist. You become utterly incapable of wild irrationality (and you probably become incapable of standing up, but that's a different story).

Eventually, you will receive a vision of the beautiful interconnectedness of all things, and you might be tempted to start singing *We Are the World*. If so, chug another beer and pound your head on the floor until the urge goes away.

The Ten Most Annoying Songs of All Time

1. *We Are the World*
2. *Seasons in the Sun*
3. *Billy, Don't Be a Hero*
4. *Playground in My Mind*
5. *Honey, I Miss You*
6. *I've Never Been to Me*
7. *Auld Lange Syne* by Dan Fogelberg
8. *MacArthur Park*
9. anything by Bread
10. *Just the Way You Are* by Billy Joel. (We'd like Christie just the way she is, too, but what about the rest of the world?)

(Note: You'll never hear these tunes in The Baja, the club we own in New York City.)

Squat

Boot Factor: 3

Despite its name, there's nothing scatological about **Squat**. At least, not the way we play. Of course, the folks who sent us this game from SUNY Geneseo (they called themselves "The Cellar Dwellers of Nassau Hall") might play a little differently, but we suspect they are sicker pups than we are, anyway.

Players take turns rolling three dice. The overall object is to be the first player to reach 3,000 points without going over. A roll of 1 is worth 100 points, and a 5 is worth 50 points. A roll of 2, 3, 4, or 6 is worth nothing, unless you roll three of a kind. A roll of three 1's is worth 100 points, three 2's is worth 200 points, three 3's is worth 300 points, and so on.

So, for example, a roll of 1-3-5 would be worth 150 points, a 2-5-2 would be worth 50 points, and a 6-6-6 would be the big enchilada—600 points.

A player can keep his points only if he writes them down on a scorecard, but writing them down means he must pass the dice to the next player. If he feels lucky, he can continue rolling and building up points, unless he rolls a zero (for example, a 2-4-6), in which case he "squats." That is, he loses all the points accumulated in that roll (any points written down previously remain his, however), and he must drink half a beer.

Here's why you would want to test your luck and keep rolling: When a player makes 500 or more points in one turn (which, remember, can be several rolls), he can write down those points and then introduce any new rule he wants into the game, such as No Cursing, No Puking, No Blinking, No Shirts, whatever. (For ideas, see the *Beer Etiquette* chapter.) Perhaps this is where our friends in Geneseo introduce the scatological variations that give the game its name. We don't know, and we don't want to know. In any case, whoever violates the new rule must drink.

The game ends when someone gets exactly 3,000 points, at which time everyone else must drink a full beer.

We Told You So...

"Beer drinkers appear to be substantially healthier than either nondrinkers or wine and liquor drinkers, according to the largest study yet conducted of health differences among people who drink different kinds of alcoholic beverages.

"The survey of more than 17,000 Canadians found that people who drank beer regularly and in moderate amounts were healthier than people who drank other alcoholic beverages."

From the
New York Times,
December 18, 1985.

Stores

Boot Factor: 3

When Pam Straut of Millersville, MD sent us this game, she wrote, "**Stores** involves the skills of memory and speed." Immediately, we thought it would be way too difficult for most of our readers.

But we tested her version of the game anyway, and we thought it was great fun. The game is similar to **Categories** from our first book. To begin, each player picks a store. Any type of retail outlet will do, such as a grocery store, a shoe store, a book store, or, our all-time personal favorite, a liquor store. Everyone must remember all the other players' stores, so it's a good idea for players to name their stores twice at the beginning of the game. If someone chooses a store that has already been named, he must drink.

A player then begins to deal cards face up, one to each person. When two players have matching cards, one of them must shout out an item sold in his opponent's store before his opponent does. Whoever shouts last must drink.

For example, suppose John is a liquor store and Nikki is a hardware store. The dealer gives John a queen, and then Nikki, a few players away, also receives a queen. (Only the top card on the pile can count as a match.) John, who is a member of the Butt-Head Fan Club, can't think of anything in a hardware store, and Nikki immediately shouts, "Beer!" (Good answer, Nikki!) So, Nikki wins, and John must imbibe.

Players should note that answers must be specific, but they can't be too specific. (This rule leads to lots of great arguments, and we had to convene Point of Order tribunals frequently [see *Beer Etiquette* chapter].) Nikki, in the above example, could not just say "liquor." She must say "scotch" or "vodka" or whatever. However, she cannot say "Miller beer" and then later say "Coors beer." Once "beer" has been said, it cannot be said again. But in a shoe store, for example, brand names must be used. You can't just say "shoes." You must say "Nike," "Timberland," "P.F. Flyers," etc. Of course, if anyone shouts an item that has been said before, he must drink.

When the cards have all been dealt, the game starts over, and players must choose new stores. (Large groups of players may want to use two decks of cards per round.) As the game progresses, players tend to forget who has what store, and it becomes harder to name new stores and new items. Pam suggested, for example, that someone pick a lamp store—how many things could be in a lamp store? Pam has a devious mind.

Stores, of course, is the ultimate celebration of capitalism, consumerism, and everything that's great about our way of life. Imagine playing this game in a communist country. If you were a grocery store, someone would say "potatoes and cabbage," and that would be the end of the game. **Stores**, like most beer games we know, makes you feel proud to be an American.

Thanks also to Marc Wigler of Ithaca, NY and Trenton Johnson of Glendale, CA for sending versions of this game.

"**There is nothing wrong with drinking if you know why you drink. I know why I drink. I drink to get bagged.**"
Jackie Gleason

Trivial Beersuit

Boot Factor: ?

All right, already. Enough of the letters to the Beer Research Department saying, "You can make Trivial Pursuit into a beer game, and it's really fun!"

Frankly, taking popular games and adding beer to them is not terribly interesting. Not only did people suggest this tactic for Trivial Pursuit, but also for Monopoly, Pictionary, chess, and so on. While the addition of beer might make an existing game more fun for a few minutes, the purist knows that beer games are only interesting if the beer is an integral facet of the game itself, and not a convenient addendum.

So, we're not going to tell you how to play **Trivial Beersuit**. Nyah, nyah, nyah.

Ten Things to Call the Authors

1. hacks
2. dirtballs
3. literary vacuums
4. opportunist pigs
5. immature slobs
6. the Dream Team
7. drooling, uncultured hoseheads
8. illiterate bilge
9. elitist Yalie snots
10. rich and famous

Bars We've Been Asked to Leave

Bar	Location	Reason
Rascals	New York, NY	Playing air guitar on table top. Bimbo took offense.
Bullfeathers	Washington, DC	Lip-synching *Midnight Train to Georgia* on top of the bar.
33 Dunster Street	Cambridge, MA	Mistake #2: behaving like normal people in a fern bar. Mistake #1 was entering a fern bar. (Our excuse: we'd been "bowling" at the Hong Kong.)
The Hong Kong	Cambridge, MA	Imitating "The Terminator."
The Hong Kong	Cambridge, MA	Ripped lantern from wall.
Regine's	New York, NY	Refused to pay $10 for a beer. No kidding.

Fitzpatrick's	New York, NY	Dancing while unsuccessfully balancing beer on head.
Hanratty's	New Orleans, LA	With under-age females.
Kamikaze Club	New York, NY	Fistfight with DJ.
Mory's	New Haven, CT	Puked on table while wearing a straitjacket.
Hard Rock Café	London	Criticized British welfare state. Loudly.
Rudy's	New Haven, CT	Poured our own beer from tap.
Metropol	Houston, TX	Tried to park American car in front.
Victory Café	New York, NY	Reclining in beach chair, then dancing with same.
Juke Box	New York, NY	Removing pants.
Clarke Street Station	Brooklyn, NY	Breaking glassware.
No Name Bar	Buffalo, NY	Throwing glassware in fireplace.
The Dartmouth Club	San Francisco, CA	Defended date's honor.
Caravan of Dreams	Fort Worth, TX	Tried to throw candy in trumpet player's trumpet.
Molly's	New Orleans, LA	Encountered jingoistic Cuban sailors.

Dexter Lake Club	(still not sure)	Locals stole our dates.
The Meadow Club	Southampton, NY	Forgot to wear tennis whites.
The Button	Ft. Lauderdale, FL	Over-zealous judging of wet t-shirt contest.

Eight Reasons to Buy This Book

1. You are tired of Proust.
2. You need an excuse to drink beer.
3. You wish to become a party god.
4. You believe in the American way.
5. You want to make the authors wealthy.
6. You want to make the publisher wealthier.
7. It beats renting the video of *Wayne's World* for the 12th time.
8. It annoys you that Garfield is always on top of the paperback best seller list.

Beer and Sex, Part II:

Beer Goggles

In our first reckless attempt at writing, we outlined the effects of beer on hormones in an essay called *Beer—The Social Lubricant*. Basically, we described how your definition of beauty in the opposite sex goes all to hell when you're really blotto. If you'll recall, this is known as "cruising the dreaded Lotrium."

Further research indicated that the chemical processes involved are much more complex and subtle than we first thought. In fact, we have determined that one's aesthetic standards don't really decrease, as we initially theorized. Rather, beer enhances your ability to "focus" on a person's desirable traits, thereby obscuring the less desirable ones.

We've coined a term for this situation: **Beer Goggles**.

The most obvious example is this: You've had a few brewskis at a party, and you notice a girl who has the face of Lt. Worf but the hogans of Claudia Schiffer. Beer Goggles will let your brain see only those gazongas and totally ignore the fact that she is a real double-bagger, perhaps even a cousin of the Crawling Eye. *But who cares, 'cuz lookit those gumbies!*

But let's say you're really fubar. We're talking blithering idiot. We're talking *triple* Beer Goggles. You're so gone that you can say, "I think you're really, like, a very sensitive person," without laughing and puking at the same time. Well, when you're in such a state, Beer Goggles can be your worst enemy, because you can meet a girl who looks like she works as an obstacle on a miniature golf course, but she has lovely ankles! And so all you can think is, "God, she sure has bodacious ankles!" You big guy, you.

This is very, very dangerous, because the next day you may actually hear yourself saying, "But, c'mon, guys, give me a break. Did you see those ankles?"

The Beer Goggles situation becomes most desperate when you can skrump a real fido and not even regret it when the Little Man with the Hammer (a.k.a. "Mr. Hangover") arrives the next morning.

The concept of Beer Goggles gets far more intimate than mere sins of the flesh, however. Yes, we're talking about the goggles' main corollary, **Foodnoculars**.

Foodnoculars usually arrive after you've tried to cruise the dreaded Lotrium and struck out. You have one, and only one, thought: food. You need food now. The brain realizes that a review of the last hour (when you actually told that walking barf bag you might be "in love" with her) could drive you to total despair. So the brain, stimulated by beer, enhances the power of your Beer Goggles exponentially, blocking out everything else, even if some obscure sector of your brain has suddenly developed an unassailable Grand Unification Theory. The real issue is, where's the nearest 24-hour deli? Or, better yet, pizza!

In these moments, we are at our most atavistic. Never mind

that the food consumed will never pause long enough in your mouth to register on your taste buds. That's not important. Late-night food runs answer to a higher calling.

After the feast, your Beer Goggles next focus on one last concept: sleep. How far is it from the pizza place to my bed? Gosh, wouldn't it be nice to lie down here just for a few minutes. Hey, the grass sure looks soft under that tree over there . . .

More Synonyms for "Drunk"

at sea
antiseptic
ass backwards
ate the dog
Bacchus-butted
back teeth afloat
beginning to fly
big
biting the brute
blimped
blissed
bottled
carrying two red lights
cherubimical
corkscrewed
couched
disguised
fears no man
feeling his cheerios
fossilized
gilded
guttered

half nelson
halfway to Concord
high in the saddle
in orbit
in The Zone
malted
negative thirsty
off to the races
pasted
phffft
put to bed with a shovel
schlitzed
three sheets to the wind
spiffled
steamrolled
toxxed
turbo-charged
tanglelegged
under the table
unkdray
unsober
zoned

THE BEER CATALOG

A Letter from the Guys

Dear Beer-Gaming Friends,

Cheers! We are delighted to offer you a cornucopia of handy items designed to increase your beer drinking pleasure exponentially! Many of these items were created by us during our research, and many were suggested to us by fans, who would say, "Hey, beer guys, how come I can't find a Table Zamboni at any of the finer retail outlets in America?" Or, "Say, why don't you guys invent a snarf recycler? I'll bet you'd make millions!"

We're so sure you and your friends will be thrilled with these items that we're offering this extraordinary guarantee: complete satisfaction or your postage back! Also, if you order by Christmas, your name will go into our big Beer Sweepstakes, and you might be a lucky winner! First prize is a case of Schlitz Malt Liquor! Second prize is two cases!

So don't delay, order today. If you have a major credit card or a pretty sister, just call 1-800-BREWGOD for fast, friendly service!

Remember, our motto is "Beauty is in the eye of the beer holder," and you, our customer with disposable income, is our top priority. Thank you for allowing us to take your money.

Andy, Scott, Ben, and Michael

Beer Goggles. A very popular item, Beer Goggles protect against traditional beer game hazards like flying caps, major spillage, power boots, and fire extinguisher fights. Special shatterproof design protects eyes, while wipers guarantee unobscured vision. Optional defroster and nose headlight for Arctic winter drinking also available. Weight: 9 oz. Code: GEEK. **$19.95.**

Heavefree Barf Bags. Don't just snarf—when you can really barf with Heavefree! Neat, convenient way to dispose of gaming excesses, and the two-ply design won't split or burst. Includes famous chin mount to keep bag in place and prevent embarrassing woofage while partying hard. Comes in boxes of 12. Weight: 1 lb. Codes: YUKE1 (one-quart personal size), YUKE2 (five-gallon party size). **$5.95.**

Pancho Villa Beer Bandolier. The secret to Villa's ability to hide for weeks, the Beer Bandolier contains a 30-day supply of beer. Perfect for camping trips, sporting events, boring classes, or fighting dictatorships. Design allows for quick draw and minimal spillage. Available in 7 oz., 12 oz., or tall boy sizes. Sombrero and pistols not included. Weight: 8 oz. empty, 12 lbs. loaded. Code: CERVEZA. **$21.95.**

No-Mess Snarf Recycler. Put an end to embarrassing and wasteful snarfs with this simple, handy gadget. Portable space-age tubing discreetly passes snarf from nose to mouth. Nose seals keep tubes in place even when snickering, hedge-hopping, or sneezing (though that's really gross). Throw your handkerchiefs away! One size fits all. Weight: 2 oz. Code: YUCK. **$8.95.**

Keg Disguise Kits. *Here's the newest technology for sneaking beer into sporting events, concerts, movies, and the ballet. Keg Disguise Kits are guaranteed to fool even the sharpest ticket-takers and security guards.*

Quasimodo Kit. Security guards will be overcome with sympathy when you wear this brilliant hunchback disguise. The hump, of course, contains the keg, and the tap is concealed in a cane. Kit includes robe, belt, cane, and black stuff to put on your teeth. Weight: 6 lbs. Code: LUMP. **$19.95**.

Drum Major Kit. When the wearer of this disguise mutters, "I'm with the band," nobody will dare to argue! Kit comes with drumstick heads, "drum" covers, and goofy uniform. Tap is used as drumstick. Weight: 6 lbs. Code: BOOM. **$29.95**.

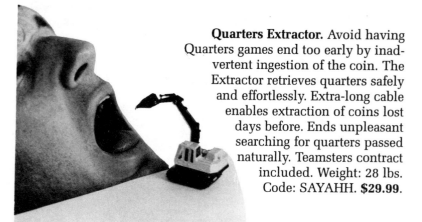

Quarters Extractor. Avoid having Quarters games end too early by inadvertent ingestion of the coin. The Extractor retrieves quarters safely and effortlessly. Extra-long cable enables extraction of coins lost days before. Ends unpleasant searching for quarters passed naturally. Teamsters contract included. Weight: 28 lbs. Code: SAYAHH. **$29.99**.

***Presto!* Replacement Brains.** Years of intense beer gaming can give your brain the acuity of a baked potato. But why use a burned-out model when you can have a *Presto!* Replacement Brain? New brains are picked to order and packed in their own creative juices. *Presto!* brains come from the top intelligence centers of the nation, like Princeton, Stanford, New Haven, and New York. (Note: Brains not available from Cambridge, MA, Washington D.C., and most state universities.) State your IQ and sex. Average weight: 8 lbs. Code: NOODLE. **$39.99**.

old brain

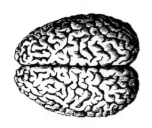

Presto! brain

LIMITED TIME OFFER! For professional party animals, we offer membership in the *Presto!* Brain-a-Month Club. Get your first brain FREE, and then we'll offer you a new brain each month for just $34.95. If you want it, do nothing and it will be shipped automatically. If you don't want it, just send back the order form. You are required to purchase only five brains a year for three years.

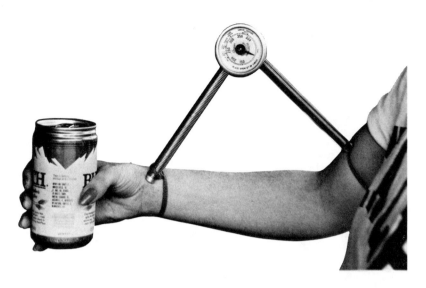

Brew-o-Meter. This neat gadget keeps beer drinkers in check and ends overindulging the night before exams, job interviews, or dinner at Grandma's. You set your mouth size and amount of beer desired, and Brew-o-Meter does the rest by counting the number of times drinker hoists beer to his mouth. Alarm sounds when limit is reached, and Brew-o-Meter locks tight for 24 hours. Ambidextrous drinkers need one for each arm. Weight: 14 oz. Code: NO-CONTROL. **$25.95**.

Eau de Beeveaux. This unique cologne, extracted from the sweat glands of St. Pauli girls, is guaranteed to attract fawning members of the opposite sex from Minneapolis to Munich. Sensual aroma arouses primal urges in all beer gamesters. One drop of this magic potion placed on the body will make your dates beg for sex, pretzels, and pizza. Available in lovely bottles or industrial strength jugs.
Codes: WHIFF (3-ounce bottle) **$27.95**, BATH (1-gallon jug) **$44.95**.

Captain Beer Headgear.
This traditional favorite transforms mild-mannered beer drinkers into party monsters! Sturdy cardboard headgear fits over eyes to guarantee anonymity while running amok and acting sophomoric. Top and bottom flaps give stability when fleeing authority figures. When not in use, Headgear doubles as a handy beer carrying case (holds six). One size fits all. Weight: 3 oz. Code: PARTYHAT. **$5.95.**

Beer Game Thinking Cap.
This fascinating item, developed by researchers at Yale, attaches to the beer game region of the cerebral cortex via electrodes and stimulates the thinking process during complex and confusing contests. Lightweight design minimizes fatigue. Advanced micro-chip makes this edge-of-the-art beenie a must for Fizz Buzzers. Weight: 6 oz. Code: IQ36. **$29.95**

Beer Motivator. Slothful runners, cyclers, and swimmers will never be lazy again! Headgear adds no weight but lots of reward, as the beer dangles enticingly out of reach. Adds inches to runners' strides. Can be worn to class or work for all-day motivation. Weight: 8 oz. Code: TEZE. **$14.95**.

Beernoculars. The renowned Beernoculars, equipped with infrared sensors, can detect parties at foreign neighborhoods, beaches, or campuses. Alarm sounds when flowing beer and revelry are spotted. Gives party crashers time to reconnoiter and devise strategy. Three-mile visibility effective through rain, fog, or drunken haze. Weight: 2 lbs. Code: PEEP. **$38.95**. *(Gumby costume not included.)*

PortaPal.
This terrific item ensures total confidence at parties or on the road. Special concave design minimizes splatter, even during a power boot. Fully portable, the PortaPal comes with rugged leather strap for easy carrying, plus a hidden drain for no-mess clean up. Available in shatter-proof porcelain or stainless steel. Weight: 3 lbs. Code: BLO-CHOU. **$23.95.**

Megabottle. A sturdy container made for gamesters who hate to interrupt contests for refilling, the Megabottle holds 1,000 gallons and can also be used to dunk lightweights or pickle small whales. Comes with handy car trailer for easy transport. 8' high, 3' wide. Weight: 200 lbs. Code: GUZLE. **$195.95.**

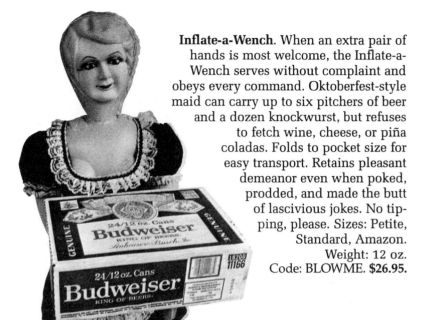

Inflate-a-Wench. When an extra pair of hands is most welcome, the Inflate-a-Wench serves without complaint and obeys every command. Oktoberfest-style maid can carry up to six pitchers of beer and a dozen knockwurst, but refuses to fetch wine, cheese, or piña coladas. Folds to pocket size for easy transport. Retains pleasant demeanor even when poked, prodded, and made the butt of lascivious jokes. No tipping, please. Sizes: Petite, Standard, Amazon. Weight: 12 oz. Code: BLOWME. **$26.95.**

Beer Shooter.
The Beer Shooter adds an exciting dimension to the popular skill of shooting beer. The spring-loaded Shooter fires full cans or bottles of beer down the throat, where they can be digested for long-lasting buzz. The Shooter can also be used to hurl beer at the fans on the other side of the football field or to deliver emergency beer to people trapped on cliffs or in deep holes. Accurate to 500 yards. Telescopic sight available. Weight: 3 lbs. Code: CHOKE. **$17.25.**

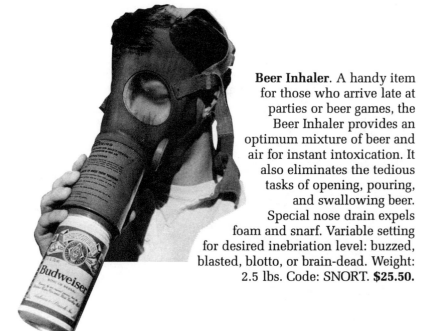

Beer Inhaler. A handy item for those who arrive late at parties or beer games, the Beer Inhaler provides an optimum mixture of beer and air for instant intoxication. It also eliminates the tedious tasks of opening, pouring, and swallowing beer. Special nose drain expels foam and snarf. Variable setting for desired inebriation level: buzzed, blasted, blotto, or brain-dead. Weight: 2.5 lbs. Code: SNORT. **$25.50.**

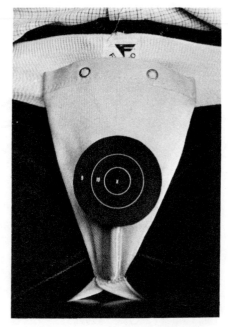

Crotch-Guard. This handsome vinyl and foam crotch protector is guaranteed to save Caps players from emasculation or impotence caused by aggressive opponents. The Crotch-Guard is both beer- and bite-proof. Unique suspension system lifts and separates to ensure 12-hour comfort. Doubles as nose-guard for dorm hockey, Bolender Ball, and other contact sports. Fully waterproof—perfect for Jacuzzi Ball! Weight: 5 lbs. Code: NO-NEUTR. **$15.95**.

Air De-Fresheners. *For that "just been partying" effect, you need Air De-Fresheners! One whiff and your friends will think you're the heartiest partier around. Patented stale beer fragrance will fool even the best-trained party noses.*

Pop-Up Keg. Semi-solid wick emits odor for one full semester. Full-bodied stench transforms any area into a post-party lounge. Includes $10 keg deposit. Weight: 24 lbs. Codes: PU1 (domestic beer reek), PU2 (imported beer reek). **$22.95.**

Handy Aerosol. Special nozzle allows stale beer particles to cling to furniture, clothing, hair, and other absorbent surfaces. Non-toxic formula can be sprayed under arms or in mouth for intimate encounters with those who swoon over party gods. Weight: 12 oz. Codes: WHEW1 (regular stench), WHEW2 (lite stench). **$5.99.**

Table Zamboni. A must for messy gamesters, this rugged machine is capable of cleaning beer spills up to 400 gallons. The Table Zamboni needs only minutes to re-surface gaming areas and provides a handy break for gamesters to ralph or whiz. Zamboni can also be used on bathroom tile for morning-after clean-up. Little driver not included. Weight: 500 lbs. Code: SLRP. **$18,595.00.**

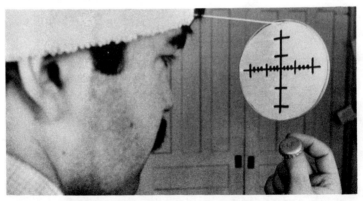

Capscope. For the Caps enthusiast who has everything, the Capscope is one more thing! A balanced optical device that offers the ultimate in throwing accuracy, the Capscope can be switched from manual to automatic to assume throwing functions when wearer is too blitzed to see. Gives range, arc, and velocity for direct hits every time. Weight: 1 lb. Code: PLUNK. **$28.75.**

Captain Leaky Statue. For all his fans world-wide, Captain Leaky, the Demon of Urgent and Copious Urination, has been immortalized in a big 10" statue. This limited edition issue, crafted by master sculptor I.P. Freely, comes in genuine porcelain. Each statue has been signed and, uh, christened by the sculptor himself. The special pedestal allows the Captain to stand proudly in his throne, even after repeated flushings. Weight: 6 lbs. Code: PPMAN. **$39.95.**

Power Straw. The Power Straw is based on the age-old technique of drinking beer through a straw to maximize inebriation. The 1.5-horsepower engine saves lung wear and tear. The engine is so quiet it can be used at bars, restaurants, churches, and family meals! Straw adjusts to pump between one and five quarts per second. Automatic choke, four-speed, with reverse. Turbo power extra. Weight: 2 lbs. Code: GAG. **$36.95.**

Beer Re-Entry Units. A direct result of space-age technology, Beer Re-Entry Units (BRUs) are designed to ease the return of beeronauts to earth after a night of high-flying revelry. Light-resistant lenses soften the blow of day and let wearer fly incognito while on final approach to brunch, class, or disciplinary hearing. Earlobe strobes pierce morning-after haze and help wearer avoid collisions with circling Lotria. Weight: 2 lbs. Code: JET-HED. **$29.95**

Beer Mite Destroyer. A versatile radar and weapons package, the Destroyer detects deadly beer mites in soggy carpets, beer puddles, and rancid onion dip. Arsenal terminates beer mites with laser-guided missiles and small nuclear explosives. Not recommended for children under 12 or for use in populated areas. Batteries not included. Weighs: 3 tons. Code: KABOOM. **$112,342.00**.

Beer Training Wheels. This handy item lends stability to beer gamers in a dizzy world. Aluminum-alloy training wheels strap around ankles to assure confidence and a stagger-free return home. No-wobble design guarantees semi-normal stride and a minimum of wooziness. Comes with satellite navigation system that automatically returns wearer to desired destination. Fog lights and air bag extra. Weight: 4 lbs. Code: VRRRM. **$47.97.**

Beer Falsies. For those party gals who want to make the most out of what they haven't got, Beer Falsies are here! The hollow Falsie is handcrafted for that realistic look. Patented suspension system adds credible jiggle while keeping beer calm. Nipple taps for easy pouring. Sizes: 34B (1 gallon), 38D (2 gallons), 42D (5 gallons). Weight: 1 lb. Code: HUBBA-HUBBA. **$19.95.**

The Beer Cart. This handsome cart—designed for travel comfort by NASA engineers—is ideal for transporting dazed gamesters to and from parties. "Kiddie seat" storage space holds two six-packs to fuel cart commander, while mesh design allows rapid evacuation of liquids or semi-solids. Top speed: Warp 7. Three models: A&P, Safeway, and Kroger. Weight: 39 lbs. Code: BLOGROCERY. **$101.29**.

Exercise Furniture. Plush naugahyde Exercise Furniture does the work for you! Ideal for the busy gamester without the time or inclination to exercise body parts other than elbow and bladder. Grainy exterior maximizes sweat production while you watch meaningless sports events, MTV, and adult videos. Patented Vibro-Gut® massager adds muscle tone to the flabbiest of beer bellies. A great his & hers gift! Potato chip crumbs and Fiddle Faddle not included. Weight: 48 lbs. Code: LARDASS. **$195.95**.

The Complete Book of Beer Drinking Games. It's been called "a classic in American literature" and "the funniest book ever written," and if you don't have a copy, your library is woefully inadequate. Over 500,000 copies in print; a standard on college campuses. Now thoroughly revised and expanded, this imbiber's bible includes 50 fabulous beer games, hilarious essays, cartoons, and much, much more. Don't party without it! **$10.95** (includes postage).

Beer Games 2: The Exploitative Sequel. If you think the first book is funny, wait'll you read the sequel! *Beer Games 2: The Exploitative Sequel* contains over 30 new games (many contributed by Beer Research Dept. correspondents), more hilarious essays and cartoons, and the wild "Beer Catalog," with dozens of items indispensable to the serious gamester. **$10.95** (includes postage).

The Hangover Handbook. With over 100 remedies for the imbiber's scourge, this book combines humor and real hangover-cure recipes that will have you back at the party in no time. Face it — if you've got a book on beer games, you need *The Hangover Handbook!* **$8.95** (includes postage).

Boot Factor 5 T-Shirt.
Now you can own a copy of the t-shirts worn by the beer authors during their research tours. These stylish shirts are specially treated for beer, upchuck, and Lotrium resistance. Nifty four-hole design allows free movement of head, arms, and torso. Three sizes: medium, large, tub-o-lard (XL). An awesome gift! **$10.00** (includes postage).

Beer Games Poster. When reading a whole book is too much trouble, try the new Beer Games poster. This huge (23" x 35"), full color print is a handy reference tool and a lovely decoration for home and office. Describes over 20 of the most popular beer games, plus gaming rules and etiquette. Whattadeal! **$10.00** (includes postage).

Boot Factor 5 Game Accessory.
Created to celebrate the revised and expanded editions of our books, this unique barf bag is sturdy *and* fashionable! Utilizing the same multi-ply construction as airline bags, our Boot Factor 5 Game Accessory won't leak, burst, or spill — no matter how loudly you "yell for Europe." A party essential, especially if you have nice carpets. **20 bags for $10.00** (includes postage).

Paintball! Strategies & Tactics by Bill Barnes. Almost as much fun as a furious round of Thumper, paintball is the country's fastest growing sport. But there's more to the game than running through the woods and shooting people with paint, and the book describes paintball's basics, as well as advanced tactical ideas that will give you and your team a competitive edge. *"Essential" —Action Pursuit Games.* **$12.95** (includes postage).

Let's Blow thru Europe by Thomas Neenan & Greg Hancock. Why spend hours in Europe touring boring museums and dusty cathedrals? Blow 'em off! Instead, have a blast abroad with this hilarious guide to a whirlwind trip through Europe, featuring wild bars, great restaurants, and hot clubs. Part satire, part practical guide, **Let's Blow** is your passport to a helluva good time. *"A temple of youthful irreverence." — Houston Chronicle.* **$12.95** (includes postage).

Bet On It! The Ultimate Guide to Nevada by Mary Jane & Greg Edwards. From slot machine etiquette to insuring a blackjack to finding the best craps odds, **Bet On It!** is the most thorough guide to gambling in Nevada casinos. The authors describe all the games, plus the best — and best-avoided — places to gamble and have fun all over Nevada. *"A book by experts — and it shows." — Travel Books Worldwide.* **$12.95** (includes postage).

MAIL TO: Mustang Publishing, P.O. Box 3004, Memphis, TN 38173 USA

Name _____

Address_____

City_____State_____ Zip_____

Phone (_____) _____

Please send me the following items:

Q T Y.	I T E M	TOTAL
_____	**The Complete Book of Beer Drinking Games** $10.95 each	$_____
_____	**Beer Games 2: The Exploitative Sequel** $10.95 each	$_____
_____	**The Hangover Handbook** $8.95 each	$_____
_____	**Boot Factor 5 T-Shirt** $10.00 each Circle size: Med Large Tub-o-Lard (XL)	$_____
_____	**Beer Games Poster** $10.00 each	$_____
_____	**Boot Factor 5 Game Accessory** 20 for $10.00	$_____
_____	**Paintball! Strategies & Tactics** $12.95 each	$_____
_____	**Let's Blow thru Europe** $12.95 each	$_____
_____	**Bet On It! The Ultimate Guide to Nevada** $12.95 each	$_____

All prices include postage.
For rush delivery (3-5 days), add $3.00. $_____

International orders, add $5.00 for Air Mail.
(Payment in U.S. funds, please.) $_____

Tenn. residents add 8.25% tax . $_____

ORDER TOTAL $_____

Allow 2-3 weeks for delivery. Payment by money order or check only, payable to Mustang Publishing. Mail order to **Mustang Publishing**, Beer Catalog, P. O. Box 3004, Memphis, TN 38173, USA. Quantities are limited on all items, and prices are subject to change. **Books also available in bookstores.**
Thank you for your order!

BOOT FACTOR FOUR

I n Boot Factor Four games, there are no winners, only survivors. At B.F. 4, the best you can hope for is to avoid being the sap who passes out or tosses cookies. Boot Factor Four competitors have applied acquired gaming skill and technique to sustain the ravages of these grueling contests. These remarkable athletes sample the bittersweet pleasure of advanced beergaming: the thrill of victory and the agony of a probable cleansing at the foot of the big, white telephone to God.

Bowling for Beers

Smurf

Brain Death

Up the River, Down the River

Slam

Suicide

The Windmill Game

The Killer King

Questions

Three Man

Beeramid

The Alphabet Game

Bowling for Beers

Boot Factor: 4

Bowling for Beers is already played by at least half the population of America. But for those of you who need to have it spelled out. . .

The most important aspect of **Bowling for Beers** is equipment. No, we don't mean those geeky bowling shoes. The key is finding one of those classic alleys that comes complete with a dive bar. Once you've got *that* crucial piece of equipment, everything else will follow.

The rules are exquisitely simple: you must consume an ounce of beer for every pin you drop or for every point you score, whichever is higher. This makes things tame if you're a rotten bowler and dangerous if you possess any skill at all. For those tempted to, ahem, spare themselves some liquid nutrition, beware—gutter balls earn the bowler a full chug. And there's one more perverse incentive: the loser buys the next round of beer *and* the next 10 frames.

Obviously, **Bowling for Beers** shouldn't be played unless the bowlers are especially thirsty. They don't call them "keglers" for nothing.

Thanks to Rob Miller of Diamond Bar, CA for sending us this game.

Smurf

Boot Factor: 4

Our readers never cease to amaze us. They think of the wildest things. For example, Mark Hults, a student at Purdue University, sent the Beer Research Department the rules to **Smurf**, a game that resembles **Hi, Bob** in our first book. Leave it to a beer gamester to take an innocent children's show and turn it into an utterly decadent beer game. Way to go, Mark!

Players must watch a cartoon program called *The Smurfs* and chug every time any character says the word "smurf" or any word derived from it, like "smurfie," "smurfish," "smurfly," etc. As Mark says, "It sounds a lot easier than it is, because those dudes 'smurf' everything."

Now, the kicker is that this fine program usually airs early Saturday morning. So, either you must stay up all night Friday to play, or you must get up early on Saturday. Of course, the latter option is out of the question, but we can't imagine missing critical hours in Na-Na Land to watch a kiddie cartoon. A VCR comes in very handy with this game.

Well, college students keep getting younger all the time. Next thing we know, someone will send us the rules for "Beer Barney."

"I've never been drunk, but often I've been overserved."

George Gobel

Brain Death

Boot Factor: 4

We chose to call this popular game **Brain Death** instead of the more common "Beer Blackjack" because **Brain Death** is so much more colorful. Also, we predict it'll really annoy Neo-Prohibitionists like SADD, MADD, GLAD, etc. They're probably reading this right now, just to work up some self-righteous indignation before breakfast.

Besides, the game only marginally resembles black-jack (you play to 7 instead of 21), and it's our book, so we'll call it whatever we want.

Playing to 7 creates some obvious prob-lems, but they are par-tially resolved by the scoring system: aces count one, face cards count 1/2, and 8's, 9's, and 10's are removed from the deck. All other cards count their face value.

Everyone plays against the dealer by betting one to three shots of beer. The dealer distributes two cards face up to all the players, and then one card up and one card down to himself. (For those of you who go to Las Vegas, this is the standard blackjack deal. For those of you who go to Atlantic City, stay away from blackjack table 23 at Trump Plaza. We wish we had.)

Each player has the option of taking more cards or standing

pat. If you "bust" (i.e., your cards total more than 7), you must drink your bet. When all other players have finished taking additional cards, the dealer then reveals his down card. If the total of his two cards is less than 4, he must take another card. If it's above 4, the dealer may use his discretion.

At the end of the hand, each player compares his hand to the dealer's, and if the dealer is closer to 7 than the player, the player must drink his bet. The reverse is also true, of course. (The dealer wins all ties.) If the dealer loses to everyone, or if he busts, then he must drink all bets.

A new dealer is selected when someone is stupid enough to ask to deal, or when the old dealer has departed to "cash in his chips."

The advanced mathematicians among you will realize that a player can bust on just two cards, which is a pretty severe screwing-over. But, hey, life's a bitch (see also "boxcars of doom" in **Dice of Death**).

Strategy tip: take four vitamin B-12 tablets and a quart of water before bed.

Son of the Ten Most Annoying Songs of All Time

1. *Do You Know the Way to San Jose?*
2. *Muskrat Love*
3. *Run, Joey, Run*
4. *I Am Woman*
5. *Midnight at the Oasis*
6. *Disco Duck*
7. *Cat's in the Cradle*
8. *I Am, I Said*
9. *Go Away, Little Girl*
10. *Mack the Knife*

Thanks to "Cardinal" Joe Potter of Daly City, CA
for sending this to the Beer Research Dept.

Up the River, Down the River

Boot Factor: 4

Of all the new games submitted to the Beer Research Department, **Up the River, Down the River** appeared most often, and, after we played it a few times, we understood why. First, this is a cards-and-beer game—always a winning combination. We also like the flexibility of the game, as it provides a fast warm-up for an evening of serious beer gaming, as well as a good respite when it's so late that the demanding mental requirements of, say, **Fizz Buzz**, are out of the question.

Equipment and Fundamentals of Play

The equipment necessary for **Up the River, Down the River** consists of a deck of cards and the inevitable vast quantities of beechwood-aged liquid. As usual, a table is helpful but not essential.

The game begins as each player receives four cards face up. The dealer next announces the "Game Status," which is one of the instructions from the following list: Take 1, Take 2, Take 3, Take 4, Give 4, Give 3, Give 2, Give 1. (Please note that the Game Status must follow this exact order, so that after "Give 1" you go back to "Take 1," and so on.)

Once the Game Status is established, the dealer begins by turning over the top card on the deck. If this card forms a pair with a card in any player's hand, that player must follow the instructions previously announced. The Game Status then advances, and the dealer turns over the next card. If the card does not form a pair, then the Game Status remains unchanged and the dealer turns over the next card. Note that each player keeps only the four cards originally dealt.

Was Up the River, Down the River *created during the filming of this scene from* Apocalypse, Now?

Explanation of Game Status Instructions

You've no doubt noticed that each Game Status instruction consists of a command and a number. The brew wizards out there will already have guessed that the number refers to the number of swallows of beer that players must imbibe. The command, of course, refers to whether you must drink those beers or give them to a fellow player.

Basically, the "Take" command means that fate has dealt you a bad hand. Note, too, that the command is in effect for each player who can make a pair with the card in play. Multiple pairs mean multiple drinkers. Further, the same concept applies to multiple pairs within a single hand. For example, suppose the Game Status is "Take 4," and you already have a pair of 6's in your hand. If the dealer turns over another 6, you must quaff eight units of nectar or face the ire of the Beer Gods.

However, of course, if the Game Status were in its "Give"

phase and the dealer turned over that third 6, you will have a golden opportunity to hose someone big time. Who laughed loudest the last time you had to drink? Who made a rude remark about your spare tire? Who was last seen in a fern bar putting the moves on a Lotrial specimen? That's your victim. During the "Give" phase, anything goes (except for pointing with a finger, of course). However, the right to "Give" does not include the right to give away beers already given to you.

A Philosophical Aside, Which You May Skip

You may ask, "Why is this game called **Up the River, Down the River**?" (And if you can say it using boldface words, you *are* a Beer God.) In a general sense, the name applies to the river of beer you'll consume and the process of counting from one to four and back to one.

But we suspect that Francis Ford Coppola invented this game while filming *Apocalypse, Now*. Think about it: the journey up a river, danger from brooding fate and the machinations of your colleagues, a bald, fat guy grunting poetry from T.S. Eliot. And the next day, you can survey the remains and shout, "I love the smell of stale beer in the morning! It smells like . . . somebody yorked."

We say Boot Factor Four, and to all the readers who sent us this game, a job well done.

> **"It provokes the desire, but it takes away the performance."**
> **William Shakespeare,**
> ***Macbeth***

Slam

Boot Factor: 4

And now, from the Beavis School for Beer Sophisticates and Jim Rich of Burlington, VT, we bring you **Slam**. Read this carefully; you might miss something.

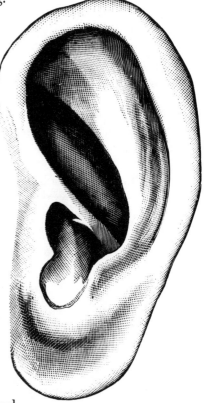

Slam must be played by two teams with at least three players each. A member of Team 1 has a quarter hidden in his palm. His teammates know who has the quarter, but Team 2 is clueless.

On the count of three, all players of Team 1 must slam their palms on the table and leave them there. The members of Team 2 must use their aural acuity (i.e., hearing) to determine which hands the quarter is *not* in. These hands are lifted one at a time until the quarter is revealed. Each member of Team 2 must drink for each hand that remains after the quarter is revealed.

Of course, if the jukebox is loud, or if you haven't cleaned your ears in a while, **Slam** can be punishing.

For best results, we recommend playing on your parents' crystal dining table. The tonal qualities will be sublime.

Since this game involves good hearing and a modicum of motor skills, we could make Helen Keller jokes, but we won't.

Suicide

Boot Factor: 4

Suicide is a card game best played with five or more people. (A one-on-one match would make the game Boot Factor 5.) Thanks to Scott Buatti and Randall Hall of U. New Hampshire for sharing this game and some of their more depraved moments with us.

A dealer picks a "suicide suit" and then deals cards face up to each player until someone gets a card in that suit. If the suit is hearts, for example, the first player to receive a heart must drink. How much he drinks depends on the value of the card. If the card is, say, a 4, then he must drink while the rest of the players count to four. If the card is a 10, then everyone counts to ten. Jacks count as 11, queens 12, kings 13, and aces 14.

The drinker, once he has finished and belched mightily, becomes the dealer and gets to name the new suit.

For the record, when Scott and Randall wrote to us about this game, they also told us something rather shocking, anthropologically speaking. They said, "Some of us like to place **The Complete Book of Beer Drinking Games** in the middle of the floor, circle around it, and pray to it before we play Quarters or Caps."

And we thought Elvis had the only new religion getting off the ground. Perhaps some of you readers would like to write a term paper on these guys?

The Windmill Game

Boot Factor: 4

At first glance, **The Windmill Game** seems pretty inane. But we became fans as soon as we tried it. It's possibly the only beer game that can be used as a creative outlet for artsy dancer types.

To begin, place a matchbook on top of an empty beer bottle at the edge of a table. Then make sure there's about 10 or 15 feet of space in front of the table. If the floor is carpeted, you're in luck. Aggressive players may want to invest in a gym mat.

The object of the game is to knock the matchbook off the bottle in one fluid motion, beginning about 10 feet away, without knocking the bottle over. You may not hesitate or stutter in the least, and you may use any part of your body.

What makes **The Windmill Game** so amusing are the creative, silly, and downright stupid methods that players devise for their "approach." Some people crank the stereo and imitate their favorite rock star. Others do gymnastics—flips and cartwheels are especially sporting. Many prefer to try to knock the matchbook off with a ferocious Bruce Lee/Chuck Norris karate kick, while yelling something suitable like, "Ninja!" Of course, some prefer the Mikhail Baryshnikov approach, with pirouettes and leaps and such—but not at our parties.

Two more things. If the crowd determines that your movements were not entirely fluid, you must drink half a beer and try again. Also, of course, knocking over the bottle means a penalty of half a beer.

The Killer King

Boot Factor: 4

Readers sent us dozens of new beer games involving cards, but **The Killer King** is one of the best we tested. Many thanks to beer researcher Donn Williams of Watertown, NY.

You'll need a deck of cards, a pair of dice, and lots of brew. To start, the dealer (who may play or not) gives two cards face up to the player on his right. That player then bets up to five shots of beer that he can roll a number on the pair of dice that will be between the value of the two cards he has. The cards are scored as follows: numbered cards equal their number, aces are 1, jacks are 11, queens are 12, and kings require an automatic drink (see below).

So, if a player is dealt a 6 and a jack, he must roll a 7, 8, 9, or 10 on the dice to win. A winning player may "donate" the number of shots he bet to the player of his choice. (He may also divide the shots among players.) If the player loses, he must consume all the shots he bet before the dealer begins the next hand.

Kings are nasty exceptions in this game (hence the name "Killer King," get it?), because a king would be equal to 13, and you can't roll 13 on the dice. The player who gets a king must drink the number of shots equal to the second card in his hand (i.e., if you get a king and a 7, you must drink seven shots). "What if you get two kings?" you ask innocently. Yep, you guessed it—13 shots of the nectar of the gods, killer.

There are two other automatic drinks. One is when a player receives a pair (other than kings, of course). The penalty: everyone drinks a shot, then the player rolls the dice. The other is when a player receives two consecutively numbered cards (e.g., 6 and 7). In this case, the player must roll the dice and drink whatever the dice say.

Questions

Boot Factor: 4

This hilarious game, somewhat similar to **I Never** in our first book, can be played one-on-one, but groups make it much more fun. To succeed at **Questions**, you'll need the creative wit of Robin Williams and the emotional control of Mr. Spock.

To begin, all players sit in a circle so that everyone can have eye contact. Someone starts by looking directly at a player and asking a question. The question can be silly, serious, obscene, whatever. The player being questioned must respond quickly with a question of his own. He cannot answer the original question, repeat an earlier question, laugh, stammer, say, "I'll kill you for asking me that!", etc. If he doesn't ask a new question, he drinks.

While it is legal to answer a question by saying, "What?" or "Who?" and so forth, such responses can happen only once per game. Anyone who says, "What?" after it's been said before must chug. Of course, "What?" can be used strategically, too:

> ***Biff:*** "Are you a wuss?"
> ***Moose:*** "What?"
> ***Biff:*** "Are you a wuss?"

Biff drinks for repeating a question.

As experienced male gamesters will surmise, the key to this game is to play with inexperienced females or pompous, stuffy guys. Start off with innocuous questions—nothing too vulgar or shocking—to set the trap, then spring something totally outrageous: "Which hand do you masturbate with?" or "You crave anal sex, don't you?"

We must also report that the Big Question—"Will you marry me?"—has, as of this writing, tripped up three of the four authors, and they now have someone to share their penalty chugs for life.

(Thanks to Mike Niederkorn of Chicago and Janet Feulner & Tom Stanton of Dumont, NJ for sending this game.)

He's Drunker than...

a badger	a sailor
a bat	a skunk in a trunk
a boiled owl	a tapster
a brewer's fart	a wheelbarrow
a coon	Bacchus
a fiddler	blazes
a fish	Cooter Brown
a hoot owl	hell
a little red wagon	mice
a loon	muck
a monkey	the devil
a pig	whiskey
a rolling fart	Zeus

Three Man

Boot Factor: 4

Based on the hundreds of letters we've received describing this game, **Three Man** may soon overtake **Quarters** as the most popular beer game in America. Indeed, you cannot call yourself an accomplished gamester if you are not knowledgeable and skillful in this most enjoyable contest.

To play, you'll need at least four people, two dice, one goofy-looking hat (see page 78 for a common source), and innumerable brewskis, of course. At the start, each player rolls one die. The first player who rolls a 3 is the "Three Man,"* and he must don the goofy headgear.

The player on the Three Man's left goes first, and the play continues in this direction. The object of the game is to roll doubles, a 3, or a multiple of 3. Doubles gives you the right to assign drinks to other players. However, you can make one person drink only the maximum amount on one die. If you roll double 4's, for example, you can make one player drink four times, another player drink three times, and another drink once, but you can't make one person drink eight times from that roll.

The Three Man must wear a dorky hat.

*If you are offended by the sexist language of this game, feel free to call it "Three Person." Also, feel free to get a real life.

As if wearing a dorky hat weren't punishment enough, the Three Man must drink whenever any player rolls a 3 or a multiple of 3. Roll 3-1? Three Man drinks. Roll 5-4? Three Man drinks (since 9 is a multiple of 3). Roll 3-3? Three Man drinks twice, plus you can assign six drinks around the table. (Hey, the Three Man looks thirsty; why not give him those drinks?!) A player retains control of the dice until he fails to roll a 3 or a multiple thereof.

Obviously, the Three Man is a bullseye for gaming sadists. However, spitefulness, as in real life, carries a price. There's only one way for the hapless Three Man to escape his predicament: he must roll a 3 for himself. If he does, he can award any player his "crown" and his title. If you've been hammering on the poor Three Man, be prepared for his revenge.

Other dice rolls prompt additional actions:

- roll 7: player on the roller's left drinks.
- roll 11: player on the roller's right drinks.
- roll 10: social—everyone drinks.
- roll 2-1: Three Man drinks, of course, and roller must throw again to determine how many drinks he himself must take.
- roll 4-1: each player must place a finger on his nose; last to do so drinks.
- roll 4-2: Three Man drinks, and the roller becomes the "Dick Man" and must fetch beer for the other players. He can negate this humiliating position only by rolling another 4-2.
- roll die off table: roller drinks twice and must pass the dice to the Three Man.

Until now, the official rules have never been properly codified, so the letters we received varied widely in terms of which rolls prompt which penalties. Some writers said a 10 instigates a social drink; some said a 9. A lot of permutations exist, as was true with most beer games until our books came out. Well, we tried all the variations, and we believe the above rules are the most workable and the most common.

Many thanks to all the hundreds of dedicated researchers who submitted this terrific game.

Beeramid

Boot Factor: 4

Did you know that the ancient Egyptians were big fans of beer? It's true. In fact, King Ramses II (1292-1225 B.C.) once offered 30,000 gallons of beer as his annual sacrifice to the gods. (Most rulers just gave virgins.)

What better way to honor this historic event than to create a beer game with an Egyptian theme? Our thanks to researcher B. Christopher Genack of Zion, IL for sending us this game.

To play **Beeramid**, deal each player four cards, then lay the rest of the cards face down in a pyramid configuration. The top row should have one card, the second row two cards, and

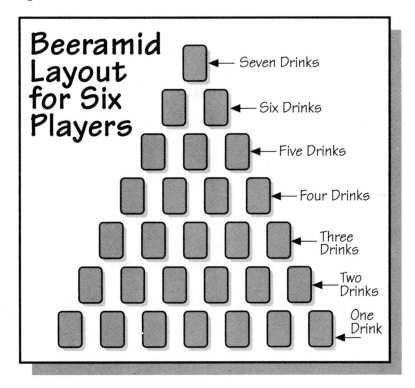

Beeramid Layout for Six Players

Seven Drinks
Six Drinks
Five Drinks
Four Drinks
Three Drinks
Two Drinks
One Drink

so on. Cards on the last row require one drink, on the next-to-last row two drinks, and so on to the top.

Someone begins by turning over the first card on the last row. If a player has a match with a card in his hand, he should shout, "Match!" and he can tell anyone to take one drink. If two players match, the first to shout wins. If there's a match within the pyramid, everyone takes a drink.

With each row, a matching player can distribute more drinks, and he can spread them around or give them all to one player. Whoever matches the top card has so much power he'll be treated like a pharaoh.

As in **Beer 99**, the fun of **Beeramid** comes in the bluffing and cheating. You're perfectly free to shout, "Match!" whenever you want. A player with a good poker face can really punish someone in this game. However, if another player challenges you, you must show your matching card. If you do have a match, the challenger drinks double the initial penalty. If you've been caught bluffing, you drink double.

Beeramid is a great party game. But don't play too long, or everyone will get mummified.

Stupid Cousin of the Ten Most Annoying Songs of All Time

1. *Kung Fu Fighting*
2. *Convoy*
3. *Afternoon Delight*
4. *Having My Baby*
5. *Brand New Pair of Rollerskates*
6. *Fly, Robin, Fly*
7. *Tie a Yellow Ribbon*
8. *Torn between Two Lovers*
9. *Rock the Boat*
10. *The Streak*

The Alphabet Game

Boot Factor: 4

Elsewhere in this book and our first book, we discussed beer's power to alter aesthetic judgment and improve the ability to focus. This strange game, developed by Carl LaFong, the former customer service manager at Mustang Publishing, will test yet another link between beer and brain: Beer might enhance your psychic powers.

You'll need six or more happy gamesters to play **The Alphabet Game**. Players should stand in a circle, hold hands, and close their eyes throughout the game. (Candles, incense, and weird New Age music will really set the mood.) One player at random begins by saying the letter "A." Another player at random should follow with "B," the next with  "C," and so on through the alphabet. Each player may say only one letter at a time, and you should place a time limit of 30 seconds or so on pauses between letters.

The only rule: If two or more players speak at the same time, the entire group must drink. Whenever the group messes up, the game starts back at "A."

It will be interesting to see whether beer affects the players' power to read minds. Does the group falter often at the beginning, only to get further into the alphabet as the sauce goes down? Or does it succeed early, getting up to "J" or "M," only to find "D" an insurmountable obstacle after a few brewskis?

Well, we're skeptics. We've drunk a lot of beer, and we can't even predict what our next phone bill will be. Carl LaFong, however, recently left Mustang Publishing for a lucrative job with the Psychic Friends Network. Call him on his "900" number if you discover anything unusual.

---

10 Things to Do
When You're a Famous Author

1. Wear sunglasses all the time.
2. Check all bookstores for your book.
3. If you find your book in the store, move it to a more prominent place.
4. If you don't find your book, complain to the bookstore manager.
5. Then complain to your publisher.
6. Take unique deductions off your income taxes.
7. Graciously agree to autograph books for swooning females and envious guys.
8. Daydream about huge royalty checks.
9. Receive real royalty checks.
10. Complain to your publisher when you receive real royalty checks.

CUTESY LITTLE SPECIALTY FOOD SHOPS

Anyone who has spent five minutes in a major U.S. city during the last few years couldn't help but notice a new blight on the urban landscape—cutesy little specialty food shops.

Like the dreaded fern bar (see our first book), these trendy bits of bilge are a symptom of urban gentrification gone mad. And what makes them especially loathsome is this: the only beer you'll ever find in these places (if there's any beer at all) is obscure and foreign and ridiculously expensive. It's never a beer gamester's beer.

All you fledgling yuppies know what we're talking about here. We're talking about yogurt and Italian ice cream shops. We're talking about gourmet coffee, cookie, and pizza places (imagine, duck and shrimp pizza!). We're talking about pasta that looks like origami, bean curd that is supposedly ice cream, and fish that looks uncooked (because it is, we understand).

Makes you want to drink 16 beers, mutter something from a Clint Eastwood movie, and blow donuts.

The problem is mostly rooted in the fact that good dive bars where regular folks can hang out and drink pitchers of beer and play pool and darts vanish when the cutesy little specialty food shops, like so many triffids, slither in and destroy an otherwise normal neighborhood.

And let's not forget the Euro-Lizards who tend to populate such trendy neighborhoods. These odious sub-humans are actually insulted if they pay less than $5.00 for a beer (that is,

Recipe for Trendy Neighborhood, Wretched Variety

Serves 10,000-15,000

1. Take one Benetton, one Gap, one David's Cookies, one gelato/espresso shop, one completely useless bathroom-stuff store (Towels 'n More), and one unisex boutique.

2. Stir above vigorously with fern bars and young adults in foreign clothing and sunglasses.

3. Remove all reminders of the old neighborhood, such as Chinese laundries, shoe repair shops, green grocers, and poor people. (Occasionally, a wino may be left behind for aesthetic counterpoint.)

4. Add automatic bank tellers, which are pumped by people before they visit the establishments in #1.

if they drink beer at all; usually, they drink some froufrou bottled water). They also angle their collars at the sky and wear stupid-looking pointy shoes. They are to be shunned by real beer drinkers, as are cutesy little specialty food shops.

THE HANGOVER QUIZ

Feeling rough after a night of beer gaming? Take this simple test to see how hung over you really are. Check the boxes that describe your symptoms, add up the points, and refer to the key on page 119 for your diagnosis.

- ❏ splitting headache — 2
- ❏ pounding headache — 1
- ❏ splitting/pounding headache — 4
- ❏ thumping chest — 3
- ❏ furry tongue — 4
- ❏ pasty mouth — 3
- ❏ parched throat — 2
- ❏ churning stomach — 2
- ❏ heartburn — 1
- ❏ wooziness — 2
- ❏ dizziness — 3
- ❏ over-sensitivity to light, sound, touch — 5
- ❏ no sensitivity to light, sound, touch — 10
- ❏ bloodshot eyes — 3
- ❏ simultaneous depression and anxiety — 4
- ❏ constipation with intermittent diarrhea — 4
- ❏ insatiable thirst — 4
- ❏ ringing ears — 3

- ❏ no sense of taste — 0*
- ❏ no sense of smell — 5
- ❏ no sense of gravity — 10
- ❏ monkey breath — 0 (who doesn't have it in the morning?)
- ❏ throat and nasal burn — 4
- ❏ memory lapses — 5
- ❏ German army marched through mouth — 4
- ❏ Iraqi army marched through mouth — 8
- ❏ electric-cattle-prod-in-the-eye sensation — 4
- ❏ brain will slip out of ear if you lean over — 4
- ❏ brain already on floor — 10
- ❏ lack of coherence — 4
- ❏ lack of speech — 8
- ❏ lack of breathing — 10

A given, since you bought this book.

- ❏ little man with hammer inside your skull — 3
- ❏ prefer classical music to rock — 3
- ❏ dry heaves — 5
- ❏ you vomit — 6
- ❏ you vomit again — 8
- ❏ and again — 10
- ❏ tongue velcroed to roof of mouth — 5

Scoring Key

If your score is...

0-10   You're probably just coming down with
            a cold.

11-30   Something got hold of you. Take vitamins
            and rest.

31-60   You are assuredly hung over. Take vitamins,
            aspirin, and mouthwash. Reset alarm.

61-90   Down a warm beer, draw the shades, and kiss
            the day goodbye.

91-120 Lie very still. You may only be dreaming. Vow
            never to drink again.

over 121 Can you say "911"?

"We could not now take time for further
search or considerations, our victuals
being spent, especially our beer."

— from the *Pilgrims' Journal*
aboard the *Mayflower,* explaining why
they landed at Plymouth Rock
instead of continuing to Virginia

A Nice Little Story

One day, I was riding on this really crowded bus when I started to feel pretty rotten. I had consumed a lot of brew and pizza the night before, and my stomach was alerting me that it wasn't all digested yet. In fact, it was obvious that I was going to blow chow.

Now, under more spacious circumstances, I would have welcomed a good earl. Unfortunately, the several dozen passengers with me on the bus would undoubtedly disagree. So, I decided that whatever happened, I would just have to keep my mouth closed. No chow could escape my lips. It was a risky decision, but I had little choice. I was feeling worse every second.

I upchucked a little bit and managed to hold it. I prayed that no one would try to start a conversation.

A little more came up, and my cheeks began to swell like tandem balloons. If someone had told a joke, it would have been all over. Power boot. In any case, I knew that one more addition to the formidable buick parked in my mouth would drive that sucker right out the garage door — and all over my fellow passengers.

As if the cavalry had come over the hill, the bus reached my stop. I scurried out the door and hurled all over the faces of the "Action News" crew advertised on the side of the bus. I just love happy endings, don't you?

THE BEER FINAL

In our first book, we had a large section called "The Beer Curriculum," which was a full semester of college courses based on—what else?—beer. Most of you have studied those courses, we trust, and now you're ready to take The Beer Final. You did bring two #2 pencils, didn't you?

1. The best thing in life is
   a. Drew Barrymore.
   b. skrocking on the beach.
   c. pitchers on the house.
   d. visiting Captain Leaky when you really, really have to.

2. The worst thing in life is
   a. missing your daily nap.
   b. Congress deciding to reduce the deficit by taxing beer.
   c. being hung over and ralph-ready on the subway.
   d. waking up to discover that she isn't Drew Barrymore.

3. **In 25 words or less, answer this question:**
   Too much is never how much?

4. **Is this a great country, or what?**
   a. great country.
   b. what.

5. **Beer is made from**
   a. hops, barley, and water.
   b. I don't care.

6. **Visiting the Lotrium is better than**
   a. having hairy palms.
   b. nuclear war.
   c. toxic waste.
   d. nothing.

7. **True or false: MADD stands for "Men Against Daiquiri Drinkers."**

8. **I have had sex in a taxi**
   a. more than 5 times.
   b. more than 10 times.
   c. more than 20 times.

9. **This is a test of recall from our first book. Complete this phrase: "Beer makes you drunk. It also makes you, uh, ... "**
   a. horny.
   b. thirsty.
   c. famous.
   d. all of the above.

BOOT FACTOR FIVE

I f the Boot Factor Four gamester lives close to the edge, the Boot Factor Five player has jumped. He accepts the fact that the Big Ralph is imminent. His only question is when to employ the reverse drink strategically in order to outlast fellow Neanderthals. Generally speaking, if a B.F. 5 player does not voluntarily hurl, he will involuntarily barf later in the game. Such a gross *faux pas* merits immediate disqualification and, of course, a penalty chug.

Quick Draw

Acey-Facey

Jerry's Kids

Human Frisbee Golf

Bite the Bag

U Chug

TEGWAR

Up My Butt

Dizzy Izzy

Crud

The Case Race

Quick Draw

Boot Factor: 5

Sent by researcher Jay Echols of Warner Robins, GA, **Quick Draw** is the ideal way to settle heated party disputes. Has someone been bragging too loudly about his prodigious chugging ability? Did someone disparage your **Quarters** skills? Did someone try to steal your date? Challenge them to a **Quick Draw** showdown and settle it *mano a mano*.

To play, you'll need two of those plastic can-holders that attach to the window of a car. Each player should clip one securely to his belt and insert an unopened can of beer.

The set-up mimics the "shoot-out on Main Street" scene from every grade-B western movie ever made. Players stand back to back, arms at their sides, and begin pacing away from each other as a referee counts backward from ten. When he reaches five, the players should turn and pace *toward* each other. At zero, the referee should say, "Draw!" and each player must open his beer, chug it, and replace the empty can in his "holster." The first player to replace his beer is the unofficial winner, but the true winner isn't declared until the referee checks each can. If there's more than a tablespoon of liquid left, or if the ref determines that one player spilled more than a tablespoon, then that player is disqualified and must drink a beer as a penalty. In any event, the loser must chug another brew for his failure.

The game has a high Boot Factor because the winner can never rest. There's always some young punk itching to prove his mettle, forcing the winner to defend his title. After a few rounds of **Quick Draw**, the cans seem to get larger while the holder gets smaller, and the only thing the victors win is a bumpy ride on the porcelain stagecoach.

Of course, there's really only one beer to play this game with. You guessed it—Coors Light, the "Silver Bullet."

Acey-Facey

Boot Factor: 5

Acey-Facey is perfect for that time in beer and poker parties when the desire to gamble is almost ready to yield to foodnoculars. Many thanks to Rodney Leeger, Jr. of Oakmont, PA for submitting this game to us.

To play, shuffle a deck of cards and deal them one at a time, face up, to each player. If the player receives a face card, he drinks. If the card is an ace, the player drinks twice. Brutal, huh?

But there's more. When all the players have five cards, the player with the worst poker hand must slam a beevo.

The game continues until the call of the wild—or the call of late-night pizza—becomes too urgent to resist.

"Show me a nation whose national beverage is beer, and I'll show you an advanced toilet technology."
Mark Hawkins

Jerry's Kids

Boot Factor: 5

Lynn Smeltzer, a female gamester from Knoxville, TN who has incredibly cute handwriting and uses stationery with cats all over it, sent us **Jerry's Kids**. Lynn also has a really warped sense of humor.

As Lynn so eloquently put it: "All you need are seven pennies and a lot of beer." Each player in turn takes the pennies and casts them onto a table. For each coin that comes up heads, the player can force the other players to drink. On the other hand, the throwing player must drink for each coin that comes up tails.

This game will get you blotto in a hurry. There's no strategy whatsoever, so your best bet is to find some two-headed pennies. Otherwise, someone will have to start doing telethons for *you*.

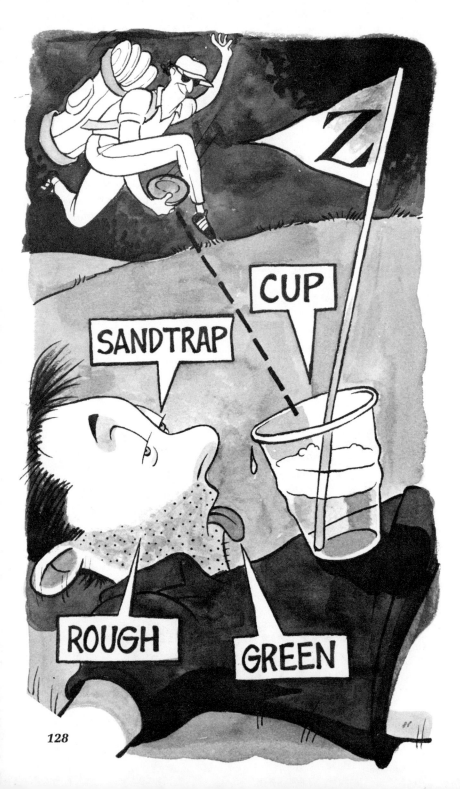

128

Human Frisbee Golf

Boot Factor: 5

Not long ago, some truly sick individuals from a college in Massachusetts—where the nights are long, the winters are cold, and the imaginations are twisted—taught us how to play **Human Frisbee Golf.** You'll get an idea of the insanity of this game when we tell you that before you can play, you must find people who sleep so soundly that you can carry them into a field in the middle of the night, lay them on their backs, place cups of beer on their chests, and hurl Frisbees at the cups. No problem. (Of course, what works best is a bunch of people who "volunteer" to play by passing out during a vigorous session of **U Chug**.)

The prostrate bodies become the "greens," and the cups of beer are the, uh, cups. All resemblance to golf or any other civilized endeavor ends at this point. What's left is a game similar to **Frisbeer** (see our first book) but far superior—*Frisbeer: The Next Generation*, perhaps.

Each player stands next to his "green," and every time his cup is knocked over, he drinks. Incidentally, since the cup was full of beer and resting on the chest of some unsuspecting vacationer in Na-Na Land, the "greens" get watered thoroughly. They won't be happy with you in the morning, but they'll be at the end of a long line.

So, you inquire, if this game is designed to waste beer by the cupful—*heresy!*—how much should you drink as a penalty? Puny human. Suffice it to say that if you pound only a Foster's "oil can" (25 ounces), you're something of a wimp. Some particularly disturbed individuals we know prefer to use mayonnaise jars of the type favored by (and swiped from) institutional kitchens (like the college dining hall). Because of the severe penalties, the course tends to get longer and longer, as players become part of the landscape.

The game continues until the Dean arrives or the President

mobilizes the 82nd Airborne Division and you and your buddies get put on Double Secret Probation.

A few strategy tips: First, never play in Minnesota in February. On winter weekends, we play only in Antigua. Such is the lot of your humble beer scribe. Also, since you are likely to greet the next morning in a prone position on the 18th green, you should be prepared for a wake-up call from some unamused constables. In such a situation, if you can't wear something appropriate for golf, be sure to be wearing *something*—or know the phrase "American Consulate" in the local dialect. A final tip to remember is that under no circumstances will the beer authors post bail for you, and we will never testify as expert witnesses, except for money.

Cheers! Or...

When drinking with gamesters around the world, use this handy glossary of non-English toasts:

Bali	*Selamat!*	Malaysia	*Yam seng!*
Brazil	*Saude!*	Mexico	*Salud!*
Bulgaria	*Nazdrave!*	Morocco	*Sahtek!*
Denmark	*Skal!*	Netherlands	*Gezondheid!*
France	*Bon sante!*	Philippines	*Mabuhay!*
Germany	*Prosit!*	Sweden	*Skaal!*
Greece	*Ygia-sou!*	Switzerland	*Gsundtheit!*
Ireland	*Shlainte!*	Tanzania	*Kwa afya yako!*
Italy	*Salute!*	Thailand	*Chai yo!*
Japan	*Kan pai!*	Turkey	*Serefinize!*
Korea	*Gun pai!*	Uruguay	*Salud!*

Bite the Bag

Boot Factor: 5

Without a doubt the best new contest we discovered since we wrote our first book, **Bite the Bag** proved to be, in our humble but informed opinions, the quintessential beer game, combining physical and mental dexterity with copious kegling capacity and great spectator appeal. It also illuminates the eternal struggle between a youthful physique and the relentless encroachment of the dreaded beer gut.

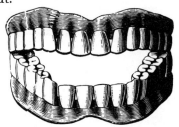

The only equipment required is a paper grocery bag (or "sack," if you're below the Mason-Dixon line). The object is to pick up the bag off the floor with your teeth. You may not use your hands, and nothing but the soles of your feet may touch the ground. Players must drink before each pick-up attempt, in accordance with the number of the round (i.e., if it's round #4, the player must take four healthy swallows). If you fail to pick up the bag, you are eliminated from further competition and must chug a penalty beer.

After each round, a referee must tear off a few inches from the top of the bag, so the bag gets progressively smaller. Eventually, only a scrap of paper will remain, and the few surviving contenders will be forced to drink mucho beer and then frantically contort their bodies in an effort to force their faces to within millimeters of the floor.

A number of tactics used in this game warrant description. The first is *The Tongue Jab*, employed when the bag is a mere scrap. Gamesters might get their faces very near the scrap, but they lack a fraction of an inch, so a quick tongue spear (like what frogs do to flies on those nature documentaries on the Discovery Channel) can draw the bag into the player's mouth.

But remember, touching the bag without picking it up constitutes failure and results in elimination.

Another strategy is **The Swoop**, in which a player gets a running start toward the bag and then swoops low to grab it. This tactic is great for impressing the crowd, but it often results in severe groin pulls and expensive tailoring.

A final crowd pleaser is **The Bag Barf**, which is self-explanatory and always entertaining.

U Chug

Boot Factor: 5

No question about it: **U Chug** gets right down to the essentials of pounding brew doggers. Like **Drink It**, you can safely say it's not a challenging game for those who scored above 400 on their verbal SAT's.

A player begins by indicating another player and stating, unequivocally, "You chug." (Our source used the word "pointing" instead of "indicating," but this must have been a transcription error [see *Beer Etiquette*].) The unfortunate player ordered to chug must drain a frosty, and he gains the right to indicate the next chugger. Of course, he may seek his revenge on the player who just nailed him, so things can get out of hand real fast.

Now, here's the philosophical part. If, for reasons of your own, you feel that some poor soul is being unfairly victimized, or if you're afraid that one more 12-ounce curl will make your date blow chunks and

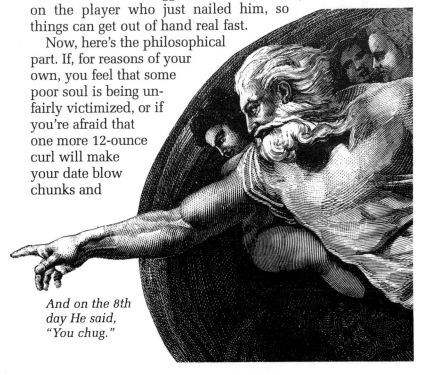

And on the 8th day He said, "You chug."

pass out, you can play the Good Samaritan and volunteer to drain the required brew puppy by saying, "Jesus saves." Then, although you're on the hook, you've got a friend for life.

We might add that any female who willingly plays **U Chug** can be described as "a good sport" and/or "an easy mark" and/ or "a beast." Let's also note that **U Chug** might make a blind date pretty interesting.

You might ask how **U Chug** rates as a precipitant of regurgitation. We gave it a Boot Factor 5 without a moment's hesitation. In fact, we even considered adding Boot Factor 6, just for this game. Don't you feel silly for asking?

**"I will make it a felony
to drink small beer."
William Shakespeare,
Henry VI, Part II**

**"The rapturous, wild, and ineffable pleasure
Of drinking at someone else's expense."
H. S. Leigh, British author**

TEGWAR

Boot Factor: 5 (for some)

Sylvester Stallone said that his ideal screenplay for another Rambo movie would contain maybe one word of dialogue. If you applied this principle to beer games, you'd come up with **U Chug**. And if you take this artistic minimalism one step further, you'll arrive at **TEGWAR**.

TEGWAR stands for "The Endless Game Without Any Rules." And that about sums it up. There are no rules. Of any kind. Zero, zip, zilch, nada. Period.

Before you start this game, it's essential that you have a few people who don't know what's going on. Your fraternity pledges, for example. Or a ditsy, but eager, date. Or the village idiot. Or best of all, find that total schmo, that complete knee-biter who plagues your existence. **TEGWAR** will fix him.

Begin the game by saying, "Why don't we play **TEGWAR**?" When the bozos ask the rules, just say, "They're sort of complicated, so let's just start, and I'll explain the rules as we go along." At this point, it's best if you have a few accomplices who nod enthusiastically and say, "Yeah, great idea!" You can count on peer pressure to take care of any doubters.

Then you just start playing, making up rules as you go along. You can invent obscure points of beer etiquette or mind-twisting variations on standard beer game rules—variations that apply only to the unwitting morons you're playing with.

You might try playing with cards. Take turns laying them on a pile. When you play a card you might say something like, "That makes a triple!" Then, as your co-conspirators gasp at the rare "triple," tell your dupes that they must drink.

Or, you can try the "personal privilege" gambit. You and your accomplices should always cheer each other's finer points of play, but if your target tries to mimic something you do, just create another rule that turns the tables on him:

"Hey, buddy-boy, let me teach you how to play TEGWAR. You'll love it, pal, trust me!"

"Sorry, you can't play a triple twice in one game. You drink."

Psychology majors will note that the mind—even the beer gamer's mind—attempts to impose order onto this chaos, and vague rules always develop so that some semblance of credibility is maintained. Even so, **TEGWAR** is the classic mind-screw. Use your imagination, and leave your integrity at home.

The All-Time Greatest Expression for

 BOOTING
Sent to the Beer
Research Dept.

Watusi with the Big White Woman

Thanks to Andy May of Parkville, MO
for sending this classic phrase.

Up My Butt

Boot Factor: 5

When Bryan Kirtley was a freshman at Davidson, he and his frat brothers developed this hilarious game. The poets and songwriters among you should rejoice, because here, finally, is a game that gives you the inside edge.

To play **Up My Butt**, you'll need at least three gamesters and lots of beer. A rhyming dictionary is helpful but not required. One person begins by saying, "There is _____ up my butt." The next player must say the same thing, substituting a word that rhymes with what the first player claimed was in his anal canal. For example, a round might go like this:

Player 1: "There is a rattle up my butt."
Player 2: "There is a battle up my butt."
Player 3: "There are cattle up my butt."
Player 4: "There is Seattle up my butt."
Player 5: "Uhhhh..."

At this point, you might assume that Player 5 must drink for his inability to rhyme. Oh, contraire. Player 5 can escape his penalty by challenging Player 4 to rhyme "Seattle." If he can't, then Player 4 drinks. If he can, then Player 5 must chug two brews: one for his poor vocabulary, and one for his pathetic challenge. This challenge rule prevents some smart ass from starting the game with "There is an orange up my butt" or some other unrhymable word.

Obviously, players must give considerable flexibility to the rhymes. In the above example, Player 5 could have said, "There is Fiddle Faddle up my butt" and been OK. Disputes, as always, should be settled by calling a Point of Order tribunal.

Dizzy Izzy

Boot Factor: 5

Also known as "Izzy Dizzy," this game will turn everything around for you. Bed-whirlies may be bad, but not even a foot on the floor and a hand on the wall can save you from the aftermath of **Dizzy Izzy**.

The game is really just a relay race between two or more teams, ideally played on a football field. A player must chug a beer and then dash to a baseball bat (one bat per team) that has been left at a prescribed distance. Forty yards is average; 100 yards is for beer monsters; 20 yards is for beer authors. The player then places the top of the bat on the ground and the bottom against his forehead. While holding the bat with both hands, the player runs around it ten times and then dashes pell-mell (yes, *pell-mell*) back to his team to tag the next soon-to-be-sick dog.

This may sound innocuous enough, but just try to dash after a chug, a sprint, and a few spins. Even if you do manage to run, you will discover that a straight line is not necessarily the shortest distance between two points, and **Dizzy Izzy** becomes an exercise in non-Euclidean geometry. Indeed, many gamesters will describe huge arcs or even run in circles while attempting to return to their teams.

Also, after you've played the game for a while, other, er, "obstacles" will interfere with the runners. It seems, in fact, that all this drinking and running and spinning has a strange effect on players' stomachs, and after a few races the field resembles a giant, beer-sodden Slip 'N Slide. Wear chunk-proof clothing.

Thanks to Ted Hughes of Fairlawn, NJ for sending us this game.

FUN BEER FACT

Mark your calendars: The first week of June is American Beer Week.

Crud

Boot Factor: 5

According to beer researcher Jon Aho, **Crud** "combines all the reasons for going to a bar: catching a buzz, playing pool, and getting into brawls." Of course, Jon forgot the most important reason—scoping the opposite sex—but we don't think **Crud** players are real successful in that department anyway.

Regardless, **Crud** is a boisterous game, best played by mosh pit regulars in a frat house soon to be condemned by the building inspector. You can try playing in a bar, but we bet "Tiny" the bouncer won't let you play for long.

Another name for this game could be "Combat Eightball." You need four players, a pool table, and mucho cerveza. You don't need pool cues. In fact, it's a good idea to lock all the cues in a closet. To begin, a player rolls the cue ball toward the racked balls. After the break, the next player must grab the cue before it stops rolling and try to sink a ball by rolling the cue at it. The cue ball must never leave the table.

As soon as the player has grabbed the cue ball, he is fair game. Opponents may physically harass him as much as they wish, using only

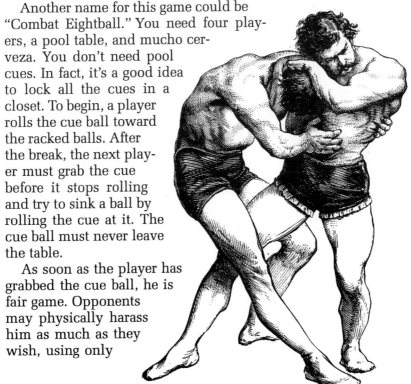

shoulder blocks to inflict bodily harm—no arms, legs, fists, elbows, pool cues (now you know why we told you to lock them up), etc. If you're playing doubles, your teammate should serve as a blocker. If you're not playing doubles, wear pads and check the status of your health insurance.

The game continues with normal eightball rules. One team is stripes, one is solids; the eightball should go in last, etc. You must drink one swallow of beer for every point on the ball your opponent sinks (i.e., the 10-ball means you drink 10 swallows). You must chug half a beer if you commit these infractions: missing all balls with the cue ball, scratching (sinking the cue ball or your opponent's ball), lifting the cue off the table, not grabbing the cue while it's still moving. If you sink the eightball, your opponents must down a full frostie.

In addition to pool strategy, **Crud** players must factor in brawling strategy, too. First, it's key to pick the biggest guy to be on your team. Second, you must time your hits to instill maximum fear in your opponent. When you're shooting, try the *Matador Maneuver*—at the last second, dodge your charging opponent and watch him crash into the wall. Another honorable tactic is the *Mountain Goat*: when your opponent charges, charge back and hit him harder (but re-member to leave the cue on the table).

Jon notes that some bars have ejected him and his buddies for playing **Crud**. "Something about insurance and police...," he said. Well, we're not surprised—some people just don't know a great beer game when they see it.

The Case Race

Boot Factor: 5

Leave it to our Delta Kappa Epsilon brothers to devise a brilliantly simple and devastating game. Called the "Granddaddy of drinking events" by the Dekes at Cornell, **The Case Race** requires a pair of gamesters (usually a big brother and a pledge, or an exhibition team of alumni), a case of beer, and a clock. Each team has from 9:00 p.m. to midnight to finish the entire case.

First place, naturally, goes to the team that drains the case fastest without booting. Second place—the team that finishes but hurls before midnight. Any team that doesn't finish and still yorks should hang its head in shame.

According to racing analyst Eric Neumann, teams employ two principal tactics. Either they power chug and hope for a record-breaking finish,* or they pace themselves and just hope to finish. All participants should also engage in professional wrestling-style trash-talking—liberally criticizing opponents' mothers and manhood—before the match to psyche themselves up for the awesome task ahead.

Well done, brother Dekes. You've made us proud.

*At this writing, the record is held by Joseph Gatto and Alan Gutzmer, both at Cornell. Their time: 63 minutes!

> **"Six pints of bitter ... and quickly, please, the world's about to end."**
>
> **—Ford Prefect,**
> ***The Hitchhiker's Guide to the Galaxy***
> **by Douglas Adams**

We Still Want More!

Heck, yes, we want more. Do you know more beer games that are not included in our first two books? Do you know more great Beer Catalog items that the beer-gaming public simply cannot live without? Do you know beautiful women who are dying to make passionate love to famous beer authors?

If so, SEND THEM IN!

Look, writing these books is not exactly what we consider *work*, you know? They're a blast, and we actually make money writing them. We're going to keep on writing about beer games as long you, our faithful readers, keep doing the work for us!

So, let us hear from you. If we use your game or suggestion in our next book (tentatively titled *Beer Games III: The Final Chapter*), we'll send you a free, autographed copy! Of course, if we don't use your game, you'll just get on another mailing list and get tons of junk mail. Write to:

Mustang Publishing
Beer Research Dept.
P.O. Box 3004
Memphis, TN 38173
U.S.A.